HOW TO WRITE A KILLER ESSAY:
A STREETCAR NAMED DESIRE
By Becky Czlapinski
Kindle Direct Publishing
2018

# Other Books by Author

*Love is Like an Elephant* Becky Walters
*Becoming Bea* (Silk and Steel book I) Becky Walters
*Three Buddhist Treasures in Kandy, Sri Lanka*
Becky Walters Czlapinski
*An English Teacher's Guide to Awesome Academic Writing for English Class*
*How to Write a Killer Essay: Macbeth*
*How to Write a Killer Essay: Hamlet*
*How to Write a Killer Essay: The Taming of the Shrew*
*How to Write a Killer Essay: Othello*

Coming Soon:
*How to Write a Killer Essay: The Great Gatsby*
*How to Write a Killer Essay: The Crucible*
*How to Write a Killer Essay: The Kite Runner*

Website: beckywaltersczlapinski.wordpress.com
Email: beckywaltersczlapinski@gmail.com

I would love to hear your feedback, answer your questions or read your essay!

# Contents

## Welcome to this study guide

I have been a high school literature teacher for over 20 years and taught all levels of students from struggling readers to AP and IB students reading at a college level. I hope that this guide will bring these two great books to life for you as well as guide you to an understanding of the text.

I say "an understanding of the text" because I believe there are many understandings of a text, for we each bring our beliefs and experiences to any text as we engage with the words on the page. The writer also brings his beliefs and experiences to the page while creating her fictional world. It is at the intersection of the writer's world view, the reader's world view and the characters' world views that the meanings of a text blossom.

Most students who pick up study guides are looking for help constructing meaning or writing, or both, so here we go.

The text I used is *A Streetcar Named Desire* with an introduction by Arthur Miller, New Direction Publishing Company, 2004.

## Possible Angles for Analysis

Before beginning any task, I like to know the reason behind my work. You are most likely engaged in this work because you have been assigned the reading and a project or an essay related to the reading. Your task is to look for a deeper way to engage with the text.

Ask yourself:

What do I know about this book? Look at the front and back cover to see what you can find out about the setting: time, place, conflicts, ideology.

Read some reviews about the book? What stands out that interests you? An exotic setting? A Gripping conflict? A coming-of-age story about growing up? A love story?

Thumb through the book and see what words pop out? Anything interesting?

Read the first paragraph of the book. What does this paragraph lead you to expect? Very often writers reveal their major motifs in the first chapter of a book.

**The opening scene** of *A Streetcar Named Desire* establishes many of the motifs and themes of the play. Williams uses setting to create tensions and ironies. For example, the working-class neighborhood where the Stella and Stanley Kowalski live is called Elysian Fields the blissful and peaceful resting place of heroes in the Greco-Roman underworld. We soon learn that there is nothing heroic, peaceful or blissful in this Elysian Fields. Stanley and Stella live in a small apartment consisting of two rooms, which affords no privacy once Blanche arrives placing a strain on the marriage which is based on physicality. There is a contrast between decay and liveliness in the opening scene as well. The neighborhood is busy, with constant music playing in the background, yet the building is rundown. This contrast is also seen in Stanley's colorful dress and language and Blanche's depiction as moth-like and tenuous. All of these contrasts serve to add tension.

The play also has an epigraph, a meaningful quotation at the start of a work. In this case it is from Hart Crane's *The Broken Tower,* a poem from Crane's an autobiographical work. The epigraph reads:

> And so it was I entered the broken world
> To trace the visionary company of love, its voice
> An instant in the wind (I know not whither hurled)
> But not for long to hold each desperate choice. (1)

One cannot not help but think of Blanche's arrival in New Orleans thinking perhaps she would find at last the safety and love for which she is searching only to find the hurricane of Stanley Kowalski.

**Some motifs in *A Streetcar Named Desire*:**
- Color
- Music
- Animal Imagery
- Anxiety and madness
- Dualities: reality vs. illusion; light vs. dark; clean vs. soiled; upper-class vs. lower-class; old vs. young; truth vs. lies

**Some symbols in *A Streetcar Named Desire*:**
- Bathing
- Train/streetcar

Reading the play will be easier if you know what you are looking for!

If you have none of the above, do not despair. Literary works all have common elements that can serve as a basis for analysis and a path into the text.

**Title** Very often the title of the text provides some insight into what you are going to read and has been carefully chosen by the author to capture the essence of the work.

Ask yourself:
- How may the title be significant to the meaning of the book?
- Why is the streetcar named "Desire" and why is that the title of the play?

**Setting** Every literary work, even most poems have a setting, a specific time, place, set of moral and social values, and belief systems.

Ask yourself:
- How is the setting essential to this book?
- How does the location or shifts in location contribute to other elements such as theme, characterization, mood or tone?
- What personal and social beliefs related to setting are essential to the story?

Setting is often over simplified when looking at a piece of literature; however, it is crucial to the meaning of many texts. Let's think about *Dracula* or *Frankenstein*. You may have never read either book, but I'll bet you can describe the setting as having an atmosphere of impending doom, of the plot being suspenseful with monsters lurking around every corner, and the characters as gloom and a touch mad. You do not envision fields of flowers, pink tutus and Taylor Swift songs. No, you envision dark gloomy castles, wind chased clouds scuttling across a full moon and some creepy wolves howling in the distant.

Setting is not only the time and place of a work, but also the predominant beliefs of the time. Does superstition dominate or reason? Are the characters Muslim or Buddhist? Is the country at war or at peace? Does society look to the future or the past?

Setting includes acceptable behaviors of the time period. For example, in Pride and Prejudice the characters are very formal in the way they speak to each other with even husband and wife referring to each other as Mr. and Mrs. Bennet.

**Setting and *A Streetcar Named Desire***
Why does Williams set the play in New Orleans instead of Atlanta or Birmingham? What makes New Orleans uniquely suitable to the messages of the play? New Orleans has long been a cultural meeting place in the South At the mouth of the Mississippi River, New Orleans was a strategic colony for trading. It was established in 1715 as a French trading post, passed to the Spanish in 1763, reverted back to the French in 1803 when it was sold to America. It was a racially diverse place with Latinos, free blacks, French Creoles from the Caribbean. It's port brought immigrants from Europe in the 19th century creating a diverse and culturally rich city that gave birth to music that was a blend of Latin, African, and European influences, as well as promoting jazz and blues music.

In the introductory stage directions, we learn that setting is a weathered, two-story house on a street names Elysian Fields, an allusion to the underworld for heroes in Greco-Roman mythology, leaving one to wonder who is the heroic figure? Is it the hyper-sexualized and animalistic Stanley is some poker-playing heaven? The house has a raffish charm, which reinforces the highly sexualized and charming Stanley Kowalski.

As the play progresses we see that William uses setting to juxtapose reality and fantasy through color and lighting. By deliberately choosing Elysian Fields as a name for the Kowalski apartment block, Williams juxtaposes the Classical image of a heroic afterlife with rolling, sunlight hills and crystal streams where hero's walk, talk and picnic with a gloomy, decaying, working class purgatory where it denizens are trapped in a cycle of guilt, brutality and madness.

**Atmosphere and mood** are related to setting. They are similar but not the same. Atmosphere is used to describe the setting and feeling a writer creates in a scene which in turn creates a mood in a reader. A writer creates atmosphere by using imagery that helps the reader experience the scene, by using connotative language, by using symbols, and by regulating the pacing or speed with which we read a text. Setting includes clothing, modes of transportation, architectural styles, music and dance fads, lighting, food and a host of other details. Writers include details to create verisimilitude, or an accurate representation of reality, to create an emotional response or to reinforce a motif and thereby a theme.

**Atmosphere and mood in *A Streetcar Named Desire***
The setting evokes a lively, carefree mood; however, the multiple dualities in the play enhance the tension that develops immediately between Stanley and Blanche.

**Plot** All literary works, even many poems, include plot: a series of
          events
and conflicts that create tension, develop character and end in some form of resolution – though often not to our expectations or liking.

Ask yourself:
- What are some of the conflicts the main character faces?
- Are the conflicts internal or of conscience or character?
- Are the conflicts external conflicts between the main character and others?
- Is the main character challenged by forces of nature beyond her control?
- By societal expectations or biases that conflict with his inner beliefs?

**Plot in *A Streetcar Named Desire* :** The play follows a standard plot arc with exposition, rising action including conflict and complication, climax and falling action. While there is a great deal of violence in the play, most of the conflict is within the hearts and minds of the lead characters.

You will find an act-by-act summary with analysis in a separate chapter.

**Character** Most good literature pulls at our heartstrings making us empathize with characters because we can see ourselves in their situation. Many memorable characters struggle and grow as a result of the plot. Some triumph while others fail.

Ask yourself:
- Has the main character grown in her outlook, ability to interact with the world, or understanding of the world as a result of the conflicts, complications, and tensions of the plot?
- Does an absent character exert an influence over the main character and what is the effect of this absent character on the story?
- What bugs you about the main character and do you think the writer created this annoying attribute on purpose and to what end?

What about the antagonist?
- Is the villain a stock character or well-rounded and believable?
- What is your reaction to the antagonist and how does that affect your understanding of the text?

Many classical dramas followed the Aristotelean unities and the ideas of a tragic hero. A tragic hero, according to the Greek Aristotle, was a basically good man who
- suffers a reversal – moving from contentment to misery
- makes a minor mistake or error in judgement
- has a tragic flaw in his/her character
- suffers out of proportion to his/her deeds

- has a moment of recognition about the error and its consequences

**Characterization in A Streetcar Named Desire**
See plot summary for scene-by-scene characterization notes.

**Motifs:** Motifs are recurring patterns in a text and often appear in dualities: light and dark, comedy and tragedy, father and son, Cinderella story, revenge, ambition, threes, and so forth. Motifs are expressed in single words and used to reinforce big ideas such as theme, or to create mood in some places of a text.

**Some motifs in *A Streetcar Named Desire:***
- Color
- Music
- Animal Imagery
- Anxiety and madness
- Dualities: reality vs. illusion; light vs. dark; clean vs. soiled; upper-class vs. lower-class; old vs. young; truth vs. lies

Ask yourself:
- Why does this image keep repeating?
- How does this motif underscore meaning or theme (more about theme later)?

Your task as a reader and writer is to determine how these motifs create meaning or a theme for the play as a whole.

**Symbol:** A symbol is an object that stands for itself but also represents something intangible or an idea or concept as well.

**Some symbols in *A Streetcar Named Desire:***
- Bathing
- Train/streetcar

## Theme and theme statement

Theme is the message of the book. Title, setting, plot, character, narrative voice, point of view and motif all contribute to theme. Theme is the life lesson or the "so what?" of a book. Theme makes a statement about what it means to be a human.

Ask yourself:
- Why do I care about what happens to the characters in the book?
- What does their experience have to do with me?

## Theme and *A Streetcar Named Desire*

What does the tension between reality versus fantasy have to say about the human condition in this play? Blanche believes she is doing people a favor by perpetuating fantasy and protecting them from reality, while Stanley has no time for fantasy and wants his reality only. Stella is more aligned with Stanley but can understand why Blanche lives in a fantasy world that is somehow kinder that the harsh real world. Is Stanley a model for good behavior? Is Blanche? Is Stella? Blanche, the romantic dreamer who lives in a fantasy world is taken to a mental hospital while Stanley the realist continues on with his life as if nothing has happened.

Coming up with a **theme statement** is a process. Since I like to trace motifs, I use motifs to create theme.

Motif: Fantasy versus Reality
- EX: Living in a fantasy world is a sign of madness.
  - Pretty basic, no?
- EX: Fantasies protect us from the harsh reality of the world.
  - A little more sophisticated.
- EX: One needs to leave fantasy behind and face reality in order to succeed.

Motif: Animal Imagery
- EX: Stanley behaves like a caveman.
  - o Pretty basic.
- EX: Williams depicts Staley as a caveman as a contrast to Blanche's gentility.
  - o A little more sophisticated.
- EX: Williams explores survival of the fittest in the new South by depicting Stanley Kowalski as a victorious, ruthless and at times savage man who defeats his enemy Blanche saving his lifestyle and family.

Motif Music:
- EX: Music is used in the play to heighten mood and atmosphere.
  - o Pretty basic.
- EX: Williams uses blues piano and polka music, two very contrasting styles, to create tension and to heighten mood and atmosphere.
  - o More sophisticated.
- Ex: Williams guides audience reaction to staged events with blues piano and polka music, two very contrasting styles creating tension and heightening mood and atmosphere.

# Plot Overview A Streetcar Named Desire

Scene One

Tennessee Williams, like most modern playwrights, includes specific staging and setting instructions for his play. Modern playwrights, unlike Classical Greek, Roman and Elizabethan playwrights, expect their plays to be read as well as performed. Before reading the lines of the actors in Scene One, we read important stage directions in which Williams establishes motifs.

The scene opens with Stanley calling out for his wife Stella and announcing that he is going bowling with the fellows. He tosses Stella a package of meat red with blood. Stella leaves to go watch her husband bowl while a white woman and the Black woman chat outside in the courtyard.

Blanche arrives looking lost and confused, referring to a paper in her hand for directions The women offer to help her and assure her that she is in Elysian Fields despite her skepticism. She is unprepared for the squalor of the place. The Black woman offers to go fetch Stella, and Eunice, the landlady, lets Blanche into the apartment. Blanche, due to her anxiety, does not want to engage in conversation with Eunice and behaves dismissively.

While she waits, Blanche has a glass of whiskey. She cleans up after herself to hide having had a drink. Blanche's anxiety is emphasized when she jumps at the screech of a cat. Stella arrives and the sisters greet each other warmly but with an underlying tension revealed by Blanche's no-stop "feverish" (10) talking. She eventually suggests a drink and frantically appears to look for the whiskey bottle she has just used. Once Blanche gets her whiskey and water, she begins to denigrate Stella's home comparing it to a house in a work by Poe. Stella thinks she is over-reacting and asserts that new Orleans is not like other places.

Blanche accuses Stella of not being glad to see her and ask why she doesn't wonder what happened to her teaching job. Stella reveals that she thought Blanche would tell her when she is ready. Blanche says that her "nerves broke" and that she was "on the verge of lunacy" (14), so she resigned. Stella offers her another drink, but Blanche lies and says she can only have one; however, we know she just had her second.

They look around the apartment which has only two rooms, a bedroom with the bathroom and a kitchen with a small bed for Blanche. Blanche is concerned that there are only two rooms and that living under such close quarters with Stanley may be awkward. Stella tells Blanche that Stanley is Polish implying he came from a large family. Stella shows Blanche a photo of Stanley when he was in the Engineer Corps. Stella reveals that Stanley travels a great deal with his job and that she misses him wildly when he is gone.

Blanche once again drags attention back to herself complaining that she was left to hold things together and watch the family die off one-by-one until eventually Belle Reve was "lost" (21). She, Blanche, sacrificed herself while Stella was "in bed with [her] Pollack" (22). Stella becomes upset and goes into the bathroom to wash her face.

Stanley arrives in the courtyard with some men as Blanche peers through the window. Eventually Stanley enters the apartment and retrieves the whiskey noticing that some is missing. Stanley takes off his shirt causing Blanche discomfort.

The scene closes with Stanley remarking that Stella told him that Blanche had been married once. Blanche tells him "the boy died" as she collapses to the sound of a polka in the distance.

## Motifs

**Music:** Williams uses music as asides, meaning that at times music is played and the audience understands that Blanche is the only character who hears it. Two types of music are featured in the play. Blue piano is a . bluesy-jazz music typically played by Black musicians at bars in New Orleans. One of the features of blues and jazz music is that it is impromptu revealing the feelings of the performer at the time. Jazz and blue music are sexually charged and evoke a languid moody atmosphere. The other type of music is the polka. Polka is a fast-paced, lively music for dancing that originated in Bohemia or the Czech Republic. It became very popular in the early 19th century and spread across Europe and to the Americas. Notice that the polka plays when Blanch is thinking about her dead husband and the guilt she feels over her part in his suicide. Blue piano plays when emotions are at a pitch.

**Color:** Williams introduces white in the color of the stairs, race: "Two women, one white and one colored"(3), Blanche's suit and pearls, a moth, and the columns at Belle Reve, the childhood home of Stella and Blanche. He also uses the color blue in the sky, "a tender blue, almost a turquoise" to add "lyricism" and "decay." Lyricism is created to evoke emotion through beauty. In the background one hears "blue piano" (3) which is taken to mean the bluesy-jazz music frequently heard in New Orleans. Stanley and Mitch are dressed in blue denim work clothes indicative of working-class men. Mitch has a package of red meat that is seeping blood introducing the color red. Is this choice of color significant? Does Williams choice in using the red, white and blue of the American flag suggest the play is universal rather than local?

**Violence:** As Blanche describes the loss of Belle Reve, the family plantation, she describes the losses as physical: "I took the blows in my face and my body" (21) setting the stage for the physical violence we will see later in the play.

**Male Animal:** The stage directions infuse the neighborhood a raw animalistic feeling through figurative language: "You can almost feel the warm breath of the brown river" (2). When we first meet Stanley Kowalski, he is coming home from work with his bowling jacket over one shoulder and "a red-stained package from the butcher" (3) like some stone age hunter bearing his kill. Stanley is later described in stage directions: "Animal joy in his being is implicit in all his movements and attitudes" (24). Williams goes on to say that Stanley life has revolved around "pleasure with women, the giving and taking of it" with the "pride of a richly feathered male bird among hens" (35). Cats screeching outside the window punctuate the sexuality of the scene.

**Anxiety/Madness:** Blanche shows signs of anxiety from the time she enters the stage. Williams compares her to a white moth; moths have a deadly biological attraction to light. Also, when she tells Stella why she lost her last job as a teacher, Blanche says that her "nerves broke" and that she was "on the verge of lunacy" (14), so she resigned. In the early 1900th century we saw a blooming interest in psychology and mental health issues; in fact, what we would call anxiety would have been call nerves, and a case of the nerves, which when it impacts a person's ability to work or function normally, is called a nervous breakdown. During this time, it was common for people with "nerves" to have a lobotomy, which involves the removal of a portion of the brain. Tennessee William's sister Rose had lobotomy in 1943 for schizophrenia, a little understood illness at the time. On two occasions in the first scene Blanche exhibits anxiety when a cat screeches and she collapses either from too much to drink or from nerves at the end of the scene.

Quotations About Nerves:

- ❖ As Blanche arrives at the Kowalski apartment, two women try to help her since she appears to be lost. As Blanche reviews the directions she has written down, Williams describes Blanche's voice as faint with "hysterical humor" (6).
- ❖ As Blanche waits for Stella to arrive, she sits "in a chair very stiffly with her shoulders hunched and her legs pressed close together and her hands tightly clenching her purse as if she were quite cold" (10).
- ❖ Blanche shows anxiety as retrieves the whiskey bottle for Stella eager for another drink: "She rushes to the closet and

removes the bottle; she is shaking all over and panting for breath as she tries to laugh. The bottle nearly slips from her grasp" (10).

❖ Stella offers her Coke with her drink and Blanche refuses, "No coke, honey, not with my nerves tonight!" (11).

❖ Stella remarks on Blanche's anxious state: "You seem a little bit nervous or overwrought or something" (17).

❖ Blanche seems afraid of Stanley before she meets him; according to the stage directions, "she darts and hides behind the screen" (23).

❖ "A cat screeches near the window. Blanche springs up" (27).

## Characterization

❖ Blanche: Williams describes her appearance as "incongruous to this setting" and "daintily dressed" in a white suit. She is compared to a moth a creature notoriously attracted to light which results in its destruction and/or death; this image foreshadows Blanche's fall at the end of the play. Blanche is quite dismissive of the "negro woman" and Eunice who kindly offer to help her. Blanche's treatment of the two women shows an elitism and condescension toward those she considers to be lower class than she. She is also very critical of Stella's apartment saying that it looks like something straight from an Edgar Allan Poe horror story. She constantly talks hardly allowing Stella a chance to talk; this shows her self-absorption and anxiety. Blanche is also very concerned with her appearance asking Stella how she looks several time. Blanche also reveals that she brought a lot of nice things to wear so she can look good for Stella and Stanley's friends. We can see that fancy clothing will be very out of place.

❖ Stella: A mild and conciliatory character who is thrust into the role of peacemaker between her sister and her husband, Stella is described by Williams as "a gentle young woman, about twenty-five, and of a background obviously quite different from her husband's" (4). Blanche finds many small ways to insult Stella such as implying she is fat, that she needs a new haircut, and that her clothes as dirty; however, Stella does not rise to the bait.

❖　Stanley: Williams describes Stanley: "of medium height, five foot eight or nine, and strongly, compactly built" (24). Stanley is also described a man's man who likes cars, games, food and women: "a gaudy-seed bearer" (25). Stanley Kowalski becomes the archetypal low-class but wise womanizer, who has a love-hate relationship with women.

## Scene Two
6 pm the following day and the women are preparing to go out to avoid Stanley's poker game at the apartment. Blanche is bathing while Stella tells Stanley about the "loss" of Belle Reve.

Stella tells Stanley that Belle Reve, the family property, has been lost and begs Stanley to be nice to Blanche because she is in a fragile state. Blanche reveals that she is pregnant and asks Stanley not to mention her pregnancy to Blanche. Stanley wants to know how Belle Reve was lost and calls upon the Napoleonic Code, a statue he claims is left over from the French colonization of New Orleans, giving husbands and wives interest in each other's assets. Stanley implies that Blanche may be swindling her sister.

He starts pulling things out of her trunk: costume jewelry, old furs, fancy gowns. Stanley says that he has acquaintances in various businesses who will look into the cost of her furs and jewelry as well as the papers related to Belle Reve which Blanche gives him later in the scene.

Stella goes outside as Blanche emerges from her bath. She handles Stanley's belligerence by flirting with him. Stanley notices and comments, "If I didn't know you were my wife's sister I'd get some ideas about you" (41) intimating that she is promiscuous. Blanche is entertained and says that she lies quite often and that "a woman's charm is fifty percent illusion" (41), but she insists she has never lied to her sister and hasn't swindled her. She then takes out a box of papers related to Belle Reve. They appear to be mortgage papers and that the bank took Belle Reve because of non-payment of loans.

In the process of taking out the bank papers, a stack of papers tied together with a ribbon. Stanley snatches them up opens the package. Blanche grabs them and says she will have to burn them now that Stanley has touched them revealing her prejudices against people she perceives as lower class. As Stanley tries to explain the Napoleonic Code to Blanche, he reveals that Stella is pregnant.

Stella returns with a lemon coke for Blanche who admits she handled Stanley by treating the Belle Reve matter as a joke and flirting with him. The two women leave for their evening out with Blanche saying, "The blind leading the blind" and a tamale vendor calling out, "red hot" emphasizing the sexually charge previous scene (45).

Motifs

**Violence:** Stanley's rage simmers in this scene. He invades Blanche's privacy by taking thing out of her trunk looking for evidence that she has swindled Stella in her dealings with the family home Belle Reve. He is angered by Blanche's flirting as the simmering sexual tension builds. He also is angry about class difference between Stella and Blanche and himself. Perhaps he feels insecure now that the sisters are together and rage is his response to insecurities, or, perhaps, anger is his response to the taboo of a sexual reaction to his wife's sister.

**Male Animal:** Williams describes Stanley's movement through the apartment: "He stalks into the bedroom" (33) conjuring up images of a predatory beast.

**Anxiety/ Madness:** Blanche shows herself to be manipulative in this scene as she handles Stanley, yet she seem oblivious to his underlying rage and building resentment. Instead, in this scene Stella seems to have anxiety about keeping peace between Blanche and Stanley and about upsetting Blanche.

## Characterization

- ❖ Blanche: Blanche reveals in this scene that she know how to handle men by diffusing Stanley's anger with flirting and playfulness. She also seems less fragile than in the previous scene. She is taken aback by news of Stella's pregnancy but quickly recovers. Blanche's flirtatious and artificiality are especially irritating to Stanley.

- ❖ Stella: In this scene, Stella is very concerned about Blanche's mental state and very subservient to her needs. She runs to the corner store for a lemon coke and is eager to keep the peace between Blanche and Stanley. Stella also refuses to question Blanche about Belle Reve and reveals that she knows nothing about papers or details about how or why it was lost leaving to wonder about her passivity.

- ❖ Stanley: Stanley's instant animosity toward Blanche makes the reader wonder what motivates this hatred. Does he resent sharing Stella with another person? Is he like a territorial animal defending his den? Does he suspect that Blanche will try to turn Stella against him? Stanley shows signs that he resents spending his hard-earned money on Blanche who has arrived broke. While the ladies go out to dinner, he is left with a cold plate. He is quick to respond, although with anger, to Blanche's flirting and pretense. He lets her know she is being transparent; however, a sexual tension is building between him and the flirtatious Blanche building tension for the rape scene later in the play. Stanley also deflects class differences by saying he will have an acquaintance look into legal matters and look at the clothing and jewelry to appraise their value.

This helps him save face. He uses the Napoleonic Code to insert himself into the Belle Reve business.

## Scene Three

Kowalski apartment kitchen living room area with poker table prominent. The stage directions for this scene focus on brilliant primary colors and the image of a famous Van Gogh painting that is a focal point.

Williams describes Stanley and his friends as "men at the peak of their manhood, as coarse and direct and powerful as the primary colors" (46).

We see Stanley dominate both the conversation and the poker game as Mitch tries to make excuses to go home to his sick mother and Steve tries to tell a joke. Blanche and Stella arrive at around 2:30 a.m. after dinner, a movie and some drinks at a local bar. Stella suggest the men wrap things up and Stanley responds by giving her backside a smack. Stella is embarrassed and tells Blanche that she has asked him not to do that in front of others. As Blanche heads to the bathroom for yet another bath, she meets Mitch coming out and they size each other up. Blanche asks Stella what Mitch does and the conversation turns to

Stanley's prospects for advancement. As they chat, Blanche gets undressed and Stella scolds her for standing in the light making herself visible to the men playing poker.

Stanley is annoyed by the women's conversation and tells them to be quiet. When Stella goes into the bathroom, Blanche wanders languidly over to the radio and turns it on. The rumba music annoys Stanley and he turns the radio off. Mitch goes back to the bathroom blaming his need on beer, but it is fairly obvious he wants to see Blanche.

Mitch and Blanche have a cigarette and, in the process, Mitch shows Blanche as silver cigarette case that was gift from a dying girl. It is inscribed with lines from an Elizabeth Barrett Browning poem (Sonnet 43 from *Sonnets from the Portuguese*) which Blanche immediately recognizes. Blanche comments on loss and illness. She then lies telling Mitch Stella is her older sister. Blanche produces a paper lantern and asks Mitch to put it over the light bulb hanging from the ceiling: "I can't stand a naked light bulb any more than I can a rude remark or vulgar action" (60) affecting a Southern belle persona. She then flirts with Mitch as he tries to determine if she is single and what she does for work.

Stanley begins shouting for Mitch and Blanche turns on the radio again. Stage directions call for a specific song, "Wein, wein nur du allein" a melancholy song about leaving Vienna. Blanche begins to waltz and Mitch moves to join her, but Stanley "stalks fiercely" to the radio, picks it up and tosses it out the window (62). Stella has come out of the bathroom and she and Stanley fight. He chases her off stage where a blow can be heard along with crashing furniture.

Blanche calls out that Stella is expecting and the men get Stanley subdued before they all collapse into a hug. Stella cries out: "I want to go away, I want to go away! Blanche and Stella go upstairs to Eunice. When Stanley comes to his sense, the men try to get him to drink coffee to sober up. He gets violent and the men leave with Mitch repeating, "Poker should not be played in a house with women" (65). The stage direction call for "Paper Doll" to be played "slow and blue" as Stanley emerges from the shower wet and dressed only in his trunks (65).

Stanley sobs that his "baby doll" has left him, dials a number and speaks to Eunice. He erupts into a rage and throws the phone to the floor and bellows repeatedly for his wife: "Stell-lahhhhh!" (66) Eventually, Stella comes out and runs to Stanley's embrace. The go into the apartment together.

Blanche comes out to find Mitch in the courtyard. She is worried about Stella and repulsed by her attraction and need for Stanley. They have a quiet cigarette together and the scene closes with Blanche thanking Mitch for his kindness: "Thank you for being so kind! I need kindness now." (690.

## Motifs

**Color:** In this scene, the focus is on the poker game and the sphere of men. Williams describes Stanley and his friends as "men at the peak of their manhood, as coarse and direct and powerful as the primary colors" (46). The colors and light are bright, powerful and bold highlighting the masculinity of the game and the players. The rest of the apartment is in shadow until Blanche turns on the lightbulb covered with the paper lantern indicating an invasion of sorts into the balance between masculine and feminine in the Kowalski home.

**Music:** Like Blanche's invasion with color and light, music and the radio serves to highlight the disruption she is causing. Williams is very specific about which music is played because the songs would have an emotional resonance with the viewers. "Wein, wein nur du allein" plants the idea that Blanche longs to be in a different time and place and is dissatisfied with her present circumstances. Sensing the pathos of the song and its implications, Stanley is angry and responds with violence as it is his home and lifestyle under scrutiny.

The second specific song is a popular one by Johnny Black. In the song, the speaker asserts that he will "buy a paper doll" that he can call his own that will not flirt with other men, and, when he comes home at night, "she will be waiting." The speaker then explains he has had a fight with his girls and is "through with all of them." The song echoes the fight between Stanley and Stella.

**Violence:** Stanley's behavior in this scene is violent from beginning to end. He becomes annoyed with the junk on the poker table and sweeps it all off onto the floor. He smacks Stella on the butt, foreshadowing their violent fight that breaks up the poker party. He also throws the radio out the window in a rage at Blanche's persistence in playing music during the game. The radio music is a metaphor for Blanche's intrusion into his life as he deflects his rage from Blanche onto the radio.

**Male Animal:** Poker is a man's game. Mitch tells us twice in this scene that "Poker should not be played in a house with women" (63,65) since it brings out men's savage behaviors. One could argue that the drinking that seems to go along with the poker game in the play could have something to do with the bad behavior. There are indications that the male sphere is somehow dangerous to females and that the danger is alluring to women since Blanche strips in shadows visible to the men playing poker (53) and Stella returns to Stanley after their violent fight with passion.

Stanley uses the term "hen" to describe women and their chatter and behavior: "You hens cut out that conversation in there!" (54). This term was popular at the time in use such as hen party, hen pecked and mother hen to describe women's activities domesticating women. Steve tries to tell an off-color joke about a hen and a rooster, Stanley gets annoyed and talks over him (48-49). Stanley is described as "stalking fiercely," Mitch's dancing is likened to that of a "dancing bear," Stella calls Stanley a "Drunk – animal thing" (62), and Stanley's c is described as "throwing his head back like a baying hound" (64) as he calls for Stella who has gone upstairs to get away from him.

24

**Anxiety/ Madness:** During the violent fight between Stella and Stanley, both Blanche and Eunice express anxiety over her pregnancy. Blanche lies to Mitch saying that she has come to help Stella through a rough patch: "Stella hasn't been well lately, and I came down to help her for a while" (60). Physical and mental illness seem to be indicative of feminine weakness.

## Characterization

- ❖ Blanche: Blanche shows a wantonness and a desperation as she undresses in a way that makes her silhouette visible to the men at the poker table. She hooks Mitch and reels him in with a series of lies and affected behavior of a fragile gentle woman.

- ❖ Stella: Much of the relationship between Stella and Stanley is physical. While Stella says that she doesn't like it when Stanley swats her on the butt in front of others, she rushes passionately into his arms after the fight.

- ❖ Stanley: This scene is dominated by Stanley who, despite his brutishness, is a complex character. He dominates the men at the poker game trying to keep them focused. He responds violent to Stella's attempt to end the poker game and reveals his raw emotion and fear of abandonment when Stella goes upstairs to spend the night with Eunice.

## Scene Four

The stage directions have Stella lying on the bed in a maternal reverie while the mess of the previous evening are strewn about the two rooms. The outside doors are open to a brilliant summer day. Blanche, filled with anxiety, stands in the doorway to see if Stella is alright and if Stanley is gone.

Blanche questions Stella about staying with Stanley because of his violence. Stella tells her that Stanley is a good man and that we all have bad habits that others have to deal with. Stella tells Blanche she is over reacting and recounts that Stanley broke every lightbulb in the apartment on the night of their wedding; she was not afraid but was "thrilled by it" (73). Blanche insist that they need to leave and suggests she get in touch with an old, married boyfriend who will help them out.

Stella tells her she is not going anywhere. Blanche then tells Stella she has no money, "sixty-five measly cents" (78), so Stella offers her half of the ten dollars Stanley recently gave her. Blanche keeps talking about how Stanley is a brute, alright for a few dates but not husband material and that what Stella feels is "brutal desire" (81) not love.

Blanche asks permission to speak freely and Stella agrees, but as a train goes by, Stanley comes in and listens quietly to what Blanche has to say. Blanche give a long and impassioned speech about Stanley and his caveman behavior saying that evolution has passed him by and real love of poetry and art is civilized. She urges Stella: "Don't – don't hang back with the brutes! (83)

As another train passes, Stanley pretends to enter and greets Stella and Blanche as they both watch Stella's reaction to his arrival; Stella warmly and passionately embraces Stanley as he smirks at Blanche.

## Motifs

**Color:** This scene is awash with early morning light and William describes a comic book as a colorful object in the drowsy Stella's hand. Hardly considered high art in the 1950s, this comic book foreshadows Stella's acceptance of Stanley and his way of life.

**Music:** The scene ends with blue piano as Stanley smirks at Blanche as Stella embraces him.

**Violence:** Blanche is astounded that Stella goes back to Stanley after the violent scene the night before, Stella says, "when men are drinking and playing poker anything can happen. It's always a powder-keg" (72) implying that she has accepted thing the way they are. She tells Blanche that Stanley smashed every lightbulb on their weeding night and that she was "thrilled by it" (73). Later in the scene Blanche says that what Stella feels for Stanley is not refined like love but is "brutal desire" (81).

**Male Animal:** In a lengthy speech Blanche compares Stanley to a caveman whom evolution has passed. Through binary opposition, setting up two complete opposites, Williams ramps up the tension, especially since we know that Stanley is secretly listening. Blanche associates love with romantic ideals such as refinement, courtesy, gentleness and artistic expression such a poetry, placing the relationship between Stella and Stanley as something other than love. Blanche's ideal of love equated with civilization and evolutionary advancement, placing Stanley as the diametric opposite: brutal, savage, unevolved. She says, "Thousands and thousands of years have passed him right by, and there he is – Stanley Kowalski – survivor of the stone age" (33) She compares his poker buddies, " Night falls and other apes gather! There in the front of the cave, all grunting like him, and swilling and gnawing and hulking!" (83) She equates romantic love, civilization, and art with God, casting Stanley immediately by comparison to something ungodly, urging Stella, "Don't – don't hang back with the brutes!" (83)

**Anxiety/ Madness:** Blanche is the most coherent that she has been in any scene, perhaps because her attention is focused on something other than herself. She begins the scene anxious about Stella after the violent fight the evening before. Ironically, she reveals her true feelings about Stanley as he secretly listens giving him the motivation to destroy her in order to protect his own interests and his family.

Characterization

❖ Blanche: Blanche further reveals her idealistic attitudes as she talks about the difference between genteel people like her and Blanche and Neanderthals such as Stanley and his poker buddies. She believes art and poetry are products of highly evolved, if flawed, people and that humanity progresses because of beauty and art.

❖ Stella: Stella is ever the peacemaker, the mediator between Blanche and Stanley, between the Old South and the New South.

❖ Stanley: Stanley, the consummate poker-player, listens to what Blanche has to say about him not knowing she is observed. Stanley gleefully hides this knowledge likely to use it against Blanche in the future.

## Scene Five

The scene opens with Blanche drafting a letter to her old boyfriend; however, she and Stella are distracted by a violent and noisy fight from upstairs. Eunice accuses Steve of cheating and from the sound of aluminum striking an object, we can assume she hit him gaining the upper hand before going to the bar down the street for a drink. Steve goes after her as Stanley arrives.

Blanche makes a sarcastic comment about jotting down all of "the quaint little words and phrases" she has picked up since her arrival. Stanley tells her that he doubts she is picking up words and phrases she has never heard before and bangs around in the bedroom as he changes. Blanche winces with the noise and asks him what astrological sign he was born under "Aries people are forceful and dynamic! They dote on noise!" (88). Stella reveals that Stanley is a Capricorn, "the goat" (88) and Blanche tells them she is a "Virgo . . . the virgin" (89) which Stanley finds quite amused and asks her if she knows someone named Shaw. The question upsets Blanche.

According to Stanley, Shaw knows Blanche from Laurel and said she frequented a dumpy hotel called the Flamingo. Blanche denies ever having been in such a seedy place, and Stanley says the Shaw passes through Laurel frequently and can double check his facts. Stanley then asks Stella to come down to the Four Deuces, a local bar, and passes Eunice and Steve arm in arm on his way out.

Blanche asks Stella what she has heard about her admitting, "I wasn't so good the last two years or so, after Belle Reve had started to slip through my fingers" (91). Stella assures her that we have all done things we regret. Then Blanche talks about how she was always soft and is beginning to fade: "I am fading now! I don't know how much longer I can turn the trick" (93). This is an interesting turn a phrase on William's part. "Turn the trick" is an idiomatic expression which means "to have the desired effect or result" referring to Blanche hiding her age with soft, indirect light. "Turn a trick" refers to the sexual act by a prostitute, and since Stanley just brought up cheap hotels and perfume, the phrase foreshadows a revelation about Blanche's past.

Stella goes out and comes back with a glass of Coke. Blanche becomes emotional and assures Stella that she won't stay long. Stella puts some whiskey in the Coke and some of it spills as Blanche clings to her, and Blanche cries out. She brushes off Blanche's questions with the excuse that Mitch is coming to pick her up soon. Again, Williams uses language that has double meaning when Blanche says, I guess I am just feeling nervous about our relations. "Relations" can be used to describe interactions between people who either don't know each other well or don't like each other: however, "relations" refers also to sexual intercourse. She goes on talking about respect and "putting out" revealing that she does have sex with Mitch on her mind. She admits she wants to "deceive him enough to make him – want [her]" (95). Blanche admits she want to use Mitch to get away.

Stanley returns to the sound of drums and trumpets in the distance. Blanche collapses in a chair with her drink and Eunice runs down the stairs chased by Steve like a satyr scene from ancient Greece. Stella and Stanley leave arm-in-arm.

Blanche is awakened by a young man who rings the bell collecting money for the paper. She invites him to have a drink, which he declines. As he turns to leave, she asks him for a light. Blanche makes overtures and flirts with the young man and even kisses him before sending him off saying" It would be nice to keep you, but I've got to be good – and keep my hands off children" (99).

Mitch arrives with roses and Blanche calls him her "Rosenkavalier" pretending she is a princess.

## Motifs

**Color:** There is little mention of color in this scene, but what there is underscores other motifs. Blanche over-reacts when some Coke is spilled on her white skirt. Remember that when Blanche arrived she was dressed in white and compared to a moth. We see in this scene that she has an attraction to young boys as she interacts inappropriately with the paper boy and says, "I've got to be good – and keep my hands off children" (99). She also talks butterflies and the need for colored lanterns to hide the glare of white light and signs of aging (92).

**Music:** Instead of music in this scene we hear the clatter of objects being broken and thrown upstairs as Eunice and Steve fight. We hear drawers slam and things bang as Stanley changes from work clothes to bowling attire. It isn't until Stanley arrives home from the local bar that we hear trumpets and drums. Blanche is exhausted by the emotions of the scene and falls asleep after her drink to the bluesy musing from the neighborhood bar in the background. The blue piano plays throughout her scene with the paperboy showing her disintegrating mental state and morality.

**Violence:** Eunice and Steve have a noise and violent fight which is treated lightly by the observers implying that this type of domestic violence is common place. Eunice and Steve make up quickly echoing the fight between Stanley and Stella in scene four.

**Male Animal:** Blanche subtly equates Stanley with animals as she tries to guess his astrological sign. She guesses Ares, the Ram; Stella reveals that Stanley is a Capricorn or goat.

**Anxiety/ Madness:** Blanche shows signs of anxiety throughout this scene. She is anxious about ageing and losing her power to attract men. She toys with the paper boy in a mild seduction, yet is anxious about her ability to seduce Mitch who she sees as a means of escape from her poverty and homelessness. She over-reacts, trembles, and becomes clingy and emotional showing that her mental and emotional stability are failing.

Characterization

- ❖ Blanche: As the play progresses, we learn that Blanche has quite an unsavory past that she is trying to conceal. Her aversion to light symbolizes her compulsion to hide not only her age and guilt over the death of her husband but also her promiscuity that borders on sexual predation.

- ❖ Stella: While Stella attempts to mediate between Blanche and Stanley, with Blanche attempting to persuade her that her feeling for Stanley are merely beast-like lust, Stella always turns to Stanley. She is not willing to buy into Blanche's ideas of privilege and gentility as her birthright.

- ❖ Stanley: Stanley shows that he is cunning and craftier than his adversary Blanche as he secretly listens as she reveals her true feelings about him. He gains a true upper hand because he has this secret information that he can use to manipulate Blanche as the play progresses.

Scene Six

Same evening around 2 a.m.

Blanche and Mitch are returning from an evening at an amusement park according to the stage directions. Blanche is exhausted from anxiety and Mitch is depressed and carrying a statue of Mae West, a sex symbol and actress of the early 20th century.

The couple approach the door and chat tiredly. Williams loads the conversation with double entendre. For example, Blanche notices the lateness of the hour (or her age) and asks, "Is that streetcar named Desire still grinding along the tracks at this hour?" (100) The use of the word "grinding" is sexually suggestive especially when paired with "desire." Mitch expresses regret about the evening, "I felt at the time that I wasn't giving you much – entertainment" hinting at feelings of inadequacy and the hesitation before entertainment in this context could be read a suggestive. Blanche admits that she tried to seem as though she were having fun because that what women do: the lady must entertain the gentleman – or no dice!" (100) as Blanche talks about gentlemanly behavior.

Mitch unlocks the apartment and they go inside where it is dimly lit. She invites Mitch in for a drink and speaks in French pretending she is Camille a prostitute in *Dame aux Camellias*, a novel by Dumas. Knowing that Mitch can't understand her, she asks him, "*Voulez-vouz couches avec moi ce soir?*' or "Do you want to sleep with me tonight?" They sit in the bedroom and chat. Mitch is proud of his physique and asks Blanche to guess his weight. He then lifts her in his arms trying to guess her weight. When he keeps his hands on her waist after letting her down, Blanche assumes a lady-like demeanor and asks him to "unhand" her (108).

Blanche asks Mitch if Stanley has told him anything about her. He says they haven't talked about her. Blanche insists that Stanley hates her a behaves badly at home just to upset her. She says he walks around in his underwear and leaves the bathroom door open. She tells him she has no money and is trapped. She reveals that she thinks Stanley is her "executioner" and that he will destroy her.

Mitch then asks Blanche how old she is because his mother asked when he told her about Blanche. She deflects the question by asking him about his sick mother and empathized with his loneliness upon her death. Blanche then tells him about a boy that she once loved.

When she was very young, she fell in love with a boy who was different who had "a nervousness, a softness, a tenderness which wasn't like a man's" (114). They ran away and got married and she instinctively knew that she had "failed him in some mysterious way and hadn't been able to give the help he needed but couldn't speak of" (114). She found him with an older man. As Blanche is revealing discovering her husband with a male lover, a train comes down the track and shines a bright light into the room.

Blanche goes on to say that she, Allan and his friend went out to Moon Lake Casino for drinks and to dance. While dancing to a polka, Blanche tells Allan, "I saw! I know! You disgust me!" Allan runs outside, puts a revolver in his mouth and pulls the trigger.

Mitch pulls the devastated Blanche into his arms and asks, You need somebody. And I need somebody, too. Could it be -- you and me, Blanche?"

Motifs

**Music:** Polka music plays as Blanche recalls Allan's suicide. They were dancing to a polka at Moon Lake Casino when Blanche told Allan that she was disgusted by his homosexuality. The music is meant to evoke her guilt and trauma.

**Violence:** Allan's suicide with a gun is the violence in this scene; a violence that Blanche lives with every day.

**Male Animal:** As Blanche describes Stanley moving around the house in his underwear, she describes him as "stalking through the rooms in his underwear at night" (111).

**Anxiety/ Madness:** The stage directions describe Blanche as "neurasthenic" (100), a general terms used at the time to mean a nervous disorder or a weakness of the nervous system. The symptoms include anxiety, headache, irritability, heart palpitations and depression. It was believed to be caused by modern life. In this scene, Blanche fluctuates from energetic anxiety to lassitude: she flirts with Mitch, anxiously questions him about Stanley, recalls her traumatic wedding and the suicide of her husband, and collapses in Mitches arms as he hints at a long-term relationship.

Symbol:
The locomotive and train have appeared in the play a few times so far. As an object, a train is designed to carry people and goods swiftly from one place to another; however, the train is restricted by the tracks and the switching mechanisms that determine direction and location. Notice in the play that the locomotive comes barreling past shining a brilliant light in the room just as Blanche is describing her short and tragic marriage with Allan. The light is clearly significant here as the past is brought to the present for examination; however, Allan's homosexuality is only implied.

Ask Yourself:
- Does this mean that society, like Blanche, is not able to face the existence of homosexuality and the related biases and homophobia?
- Is the train an image of Blanche's guilt and movement toward destruction? Or healing?
- Blanche prefers to keep out of strong light because she wants to look younger, but is something deeper at work here?

Characterization

- ❖ Blanche: Blanche finds it very difficult to be authentic as she moves from one persona to another. In this scene, she vacillates between feme fatal and southern belle as she scolds Mitch for his intimate touch one moment and asks him in French if he want to sleep with her. Blanche seems bent on self-sabotage as if she feels she does not deserve her dream settling down with Mitch and gaining safety and stability. Her contradictory behavior indicates a troubled mind and heart.

- ❖ Mitch: A single man who lives with his ailing mother, Mitch is quite the opposite of Stanley. Although he works out and has a large build, Mitch is considerate and gentle. Opposed to Stanley's raw sexuality and rough handling of the women in his life, Mitch seems inexperienced and cautious with Blanche. One gets the impression that if he had to make a choice between his mother and Blanche, his mother would win.

## Scene Seven

It is late September as Stanley arrives home to find Stella setting the table with a cake and flowers.

Stanley arrives home to find Stella preparing to celebrate Blanche's birthday. His expresses his resentment of her continued presence by mocking her bathing and scolding Stella for waiting on her. Stella asks Stanley to stop antagonizing Blanche and to understand that she grew up differently. Stanley reveals that he has some information about Blanche's past, "I've got th' dope on your big sister, Stella" (118). The supply man for the plant goes to Laurel often, and it seems that Blanche "is as famous in Laurel as if she was the President of the United States, only she is not respected by any party" (118).

Blanche moved into the Flamingo hotel, "a second-class hotel which has the advantage of not interfering with the social lives of the personalities there" (120) after leaving Belle Reve. Stanley reveals that

Blanche was asked to leave and that she had a series of short-term love affairs and was even declared "out-of-bounds" (121) or off-limits to soldiers at a nearby army base. Stanley also reveals that Blanche was fired from teaching after inappropriate behavior with one of her male students and was thrown out of town.

Stella does not believe the stories at first, but Blanche's reaction Stella's facial expression tells the audience that she is stricken. Stella tries to evoke compassion in Stanley by telling him about Blanche's marriage to Allan. She tells him that Blanche "adored him and thought him almost too fine to be human" (124); when Blanche found out that Allan was "a degenerate" (124), her world was shattered.

Stanley reveals that Mitch, though invited, will not be coming over because he told Mitch about Blanche's sordid past. Stanley has bought Blanche a bus ticket out of town.

Eventually, Blanche emerges from the bathroom and can tell immediately that something is wrong, but Stella denies anything has happened.

## Motifs

**Music:** Blanche sings a sweet popular ballad in the background as Stanley reveals the details of her sordid past as a prostitute. This accentuates the idea that Blanche is attempting to sugar-coat her past. At the end of the scene, after Blanche sings carefree popular songs, the piano "goes into a hectic breakdown" (128).

**Anxiety/ Madness:** Although Blanche seems happy and carefree as she emerges from the bathroom, she flinches as Stanley passes.

## Characterization

❖  Blanche:  Blanche's delusional pretense of being a refined, upper-class gentile woman is shattered at Stanley's revelations that she had multiple lovers and even seduced a seventeen-year-old student. This information has been heavily foreshadowed adding pathos to Blanche's willful maintenance of an illusion of not only being younger than she is, but also being a respectable woman.

- ❖ Stella: Stella is truly torn between believing what her husband tells her and her loyalty to her sister. She attempts to make excuses for Blanche's fragile mental state all the way back to her brief marriage to Allan.

- ❖ Stanley: Stanley has found the information he needs to remove Blanche from his house and life. He uncovers the truth about Blanche's recent past and is using it to ruin her chances of marrying Mitch and entwining herself in his life permanently. Like the caveman to which he has been compared, Stanley uses his strengths and connections to beat his adversary and protect his family.

## Scene Eight
Forty-five minutes later, Blanche, Stanley and Stella are seated at the table dismally finishing dinner. A fourth place setting intended for Mitch sits empty.

As Blanche, Stella and Stanley sit tensely around the table, Blanche comments that she has been stood-up by her beau meaning Mitch. She asks Stanley to tell a story, a joke; but he replies facetiously that he doesn't "know any refined enough for her taste" (129). Blanche then tells a parrot joke and laughs hysterically. Stella tries unsuccessfully to seem amused. Stanley ignores them as he eats a porkchop with his fingers.

When Stella complains that he is all greasy and "making a pig of himself" (131), Stanley throws plates around in anger. He is offended that the sisters think they are better than him and declares he is "the king around here" (131). As Stanley withdraws to the porch for a

37

cigarette, Blanche questions Stella about what happened when she was bathing. Blanche goes in to call Mitch and leaves a message with the operator.

Stella scolds Stanley for his behavior and after a few moments he takes her in an embrace saying, "Stella, it's gonna be alright after she goes and after you've had the baby" (133). He recalls how their life was before Blanche arrived, especially their intimacy. She goes back inside and begins to light the candles on the birthday cake as Stanley complains about the heat from the baths Blanche takes. She explains that she takes them for her fragile nerves stating that Stanley as a "healthy Polack" (134) wouldn't understand. Stanley asserts that he is a "one hundred percent American" and that "people from Poland are Poles, not Polacks" a derogatory term (134).

After taking a phone call about his bowling team, Stanley gives Blanche her birthday gift: "Bus ticket! Back to Laurel! On the Greyhound! Tuesday!" (136) Blanche runs to the bathroom, obviously sick at the news.

Stella scolds Stanley for his cruelty and insensitivity. Stella tells him that Blanche was sensitive and caring as a girl but "people like you abused her, and forced her to change" (136). Stanley argues that she liked it when he "pulled you down off of them columns" (137) meaning off of the gentile pedestal of her upbringing and into the normal world. Stella goes into labor as Stanley is talking and the scene ends with Stanley helping Stella leave the apartment.

Motifs

**Color:** A slant of golden sunset illuminates a water tank in the background as the city lights up for the evening accentuating the harsh reality of life in the Kowalski household and the strain Blanche's stay has had on their marriage.

**Music:** As Stanley gives Blanche her bus ticket, the polka music plays frantically indicating Blanche's anxiety; she rushes into the bathroom to be sick.

**Violence:** Stanley can no longer hold in his hostility toward Blanche and reacts violent when Stella seems to side with Blanche commenting that he is eating like a "pig" (131). He throws his dinner plate across the room and rants about how he is king in his own house.

**Male Animal:** When compared to a pig in this scene, Stanley becomes very angry. Stanley is described as "grunting" in stage directions emphasizing his animalistic qualities as he treats Blanche rather cruelly by giving her a one-way bus ticket out of town.

**Anxiety/ Madness:** Blanche is showing more signs of fear of Stanley saying that she takes hot baths as "hydrotherapy" for her nerves.

Characterization

- ❖ Blanche: Blanche knows that something has shifted because of Stella's behavior and Mitch's absence. The way she has questioned Mitch and is questioning Stella about what Stanley knows about her past, indicates that she has something to worry about, substantiating Stanley's tales of promiscuity.

- ❖ Stella: Stella is still caught between Stanley and Blanche as they struggle for dominance. She understands Blanche's history and trauma and their effect on her present. She empathizes with Blanche's psychic wounds in a way that Stanley cannot understand.

- ❖ Stanley: Stanley shows that he is ruthless in his determination to get rid of Blanche. He has no empathy for her fragile nerves and past heartbreaks.

## Scene Nine

It is later the same evening and Blanche is sitting hunched over in a chair and drinking while polka music is playing in the background. The music is in her head and represents both her guilt over Allan's death and her mental deterioration. Mitch is unshaven and dressed in his work clothes as he rings the bell.

Mitch rings the bell and announces himself, sending Blanche into frantic activity as she tidies up, putting away the liquor and fixing her appearance. She assumes an air of fake righteousness as she opens the door. She offers he lips to Mitch for a kiss, but he brushes past her and strides into the room as she complains about his ungentlemanly behavior and appearance  and blathers on about the polka  playing in her head.

Mitch sits on the bed and watches her as she fusses and asks him if he wants a drink.  She continues to talk about the polka music and hears a gunshot then the music stops.  Mitch asks her if she is "boxed out of her mind" (141) as Blanche continues to search for the whiskey. Mitch complains about the dark and says he doesn't think he has ever seen Blanche in the light, a metaphor for he secrets. He reaches up, tears the paper lantern off  the light and turns it on, so he can "take a look at [Blanche] good and plain" (144).  He wants realism and she exclaims that she wants "magic" and that she "misrepresents things" to people to give them magic (145).  She cowers under the bright light covering her face with her hands.

Mitch tells her he doesn't mind that she is older than he thought, but he does mind that she was lying. He said he called people in Laurel who verified what Stanley told him.  Blanche rants on about how after the death of Allan, "the intimacy of strangers was all I seemed to be able to fill my empty heart with" (146). Panic led her from one man to another looking for protection.  When Mitch accuses her of lying to him, she says she never lied in her heart, as a vendor goes by selling flowers for the dead.

40

Blanche has a nervous episode reliving all of the deaths at Belle Reve and how she used to bring soldiers home after drinking on the base. Mitch embraces Blanche, hoping to get lucky. Blanche asks him to marry her, but he says he will not marry her: "You are not clean enough to bring in the house with my mother" (150). Blanche tells him to get out before she starts screaming and, once she yells "fire!" he leaves.

## Motifs

**Color:** The significance of the colorful paper lantern becomes clear in this scene. Blanche uses the lantern to cover the harsh light of the bare bulb which is a metaphor for the harsh reality of the world including her fading beauty.

**Music:** Polka music playing in Blanche's head in this scene foreshadowing the tense scene between she and Mitch.

**Violence:** Mitch tears off the paper lantern in a violent act that is a metaphor for revealing Blanche for who she really is. Mitch is sexually frustrated because he is behaving like a gentleman, but now that he know of Blanche's sexual promiscuity, he wants to force himself on her. Mitch is unable to resort to sexual violence, so instead, he is cruel and humiliates Blanche by exposing her to the harsh light of reality forcing her to face her illusions.

## Characterization

- ❖ Blanche: Blanche finds her world of delusions crashing in on her. She has used lies and imagination to keep reality and pain at bay, as well as to make her lovers happy; however, the illusions are failing like her aging beauty. Blanche moves between insightful clarity and cloudy illusions with ease.

- ❖ Mitch: Once Mitch learns of Blanche's promiscuous past, he views her as sexual object. Her pretense of purity and gentility are perceived as lies, and, in anger, Mitch wants to

41

gratify his sexual urges and hurt Blanche by shattering her delusions of purity.

## Scene Ten

Later that evening, Blanche has been drinking and has her trunk open as she packs. Blanche is wearing a rumpled and dirty while ball gown and is placing a tiara on her head preening as though in front of a group of imaginary admirers.

Stanley arrives dressed in a bright green bowling shirt and carrying some quart-size beer bottles. He has been drinking. Blanche asks after Stella and learns that the baby has not arrived and that Stanley has been sent home to sleep. She tells Stanley that she got a telegram from Shep, an old admirer, who wants her to join him on a Caribbean cruise. She declares she is going through her things to see what she has that is suitable for a cruise. Stanley plays along pretending that her rhinestone tiara is "Tiffany diamonds" (152).

Blanche helps Stanley open a beer sending a fountain of beer into the air; Stanley takes a celebratory shower in the spray. Stanley asks if they can bury the hatchet since it is a big day for both of them; Blanche declines as Stanley looks in the dresser for the silk pajamas he wore on his wedding night.

Blanche puts on airs declaring that her old friend Shep respects her and want her companionship. She says she has 'been foolish – casting her pearls before swine!" (157). This is a biblical allusion which means tossing away something beautiful or valuable to the unappreciative. We saw earlier how Stanley reacted to being called a pig, and he remains calm for now as Blanche tells him that Mitch came by earlier 'with roses" (157) and she sent him off saying their lifestyles were two different for them to marry.

Stanley then accuses Blanche of lying about the wire from a millionaire friend and Mitch coming by. He then tells Blanche that she is delusional: "Look at yourself . . . in that worn-out Mardi-Gras outfit . . .

42

with that crazy crown on1 What queen do you think you are?" (158). He tells her he has been on to her lies from the beginning.

The stage directions call for "grotesque and menacing" shadows and 'inhuman voices like cries from a jungle" (159). Stanley goes into the bathroom and Blanche tries to make a phone call. On the scrim behind the stage, images of a prostitute robbing a man and dropping her purse to have it picked up by a woman who goes through it as Blanche again tries to make a call to send a telegram: "In desperate, desperate circumstances! Help me! Caught in a trap." (160). Tension builds as Stanley comes out of the bathroom dressed in his brightly colored pajamas deliberate and slowly tying the belt.

The phone is off the hook and making the only sound. Stanley hangs the phone up and blue piano plays. A distraught Blanche breaks a beer bottle and menaces Stanley with the broken bottle. He grabs her saying, "We've had this date with each other from the beginning!" (162) Stanley picks the fainted Blanche and carries her into the bedroom.

## Motifs

**Color:** Notice Blanche is once again dressed in white like a fragile moth representing her imaginary world and delusions. Stanley is in bright colors highlighting his sexuality and the real world which he represents. As we see in this scene which culminates in rape, Blanche is destroyed by Stanley.

**Music:** The raw sensuality of the blue piano is juxtaposed to the jungle-like animal cries in the background as Stanley and Blanche move toward the fatal climax of the play.

**Violence:** While Stanley is calm on the surface, his simmering resentment toward Blanche comes to a boil. The wild-jungle sounds and animal-like cries foreshadow his loss of control and rape of

Blanche. Blanche's attempt at defending herself with a broken beer bottle only fuels his rage and lust.

**Male Animal:**
Blanche indirectly calls Stanley and Mitch pigs when she says she has cast her "pearls before swine" (156). Stanley uses the expression "put on the dog" (156) meaning to dress up and put on airs to describe Blanche. The animal references in this scene are mostly projected onto the scrim in the background and through jungle sounds; perhaps implying that we are by nature animalistic.

**Anxiety/ Madness:**
While Blanche is aware of the danger Stanley represents, she assumes her southern belle persona as if gentility will protect her from Stanley. Is it the drink or impending madness that makes Blanche goad Stanley to anger?

## Characterization

- ❖ Blanche: Blanche's delusional behavior is highlighted in this scene. She is alone with Stanley, and they both have been drinking. Blanche assumes the persona that so infuriates Stanley: the gentile and lady-like, fragile southern belle. Blanche's sordid and promiscuous past makes the men in the play view her as a sexual object.

- ❖ Stella: The mediating presence of Stella is gone, and Blanche and Stanley are alone for the first time as she is in labor in the hospital.

- ❖ Stanley: While calm on the outside, Stanley seems to play into Blanche's delusions; however, he pounces on her lies and sexually assaults and dominates her.

## Scene Eleven

44

A week has passed and Stella is packing Blanche's things in a trunk while the fellows are gathered for a poker game around the table.

The poker players are chatting about luck and Stanley talks about a battle in WWII where he came out alive and gives his opinion about luck: "To hold front position in this rat-race you've got to believe you are lucky" (163).

Eunice comes in and asks about Blanche who is bathing. Stella reveals that Blanche has been told she is going to the country to rest. Blanche pops out giving Stella some instruction on her clothing selection as though Stella were a maid. Stella questions whether or not she is doing the right thing and says, "I couldn't believe her story and go on living with Stanley" (165) revealing that Blanche has told her about her assault.

Blanche comes out to the sound of polka music and asks if Shep Huntly called while she was bathing. Blanche is shocked to hear Mitch's voice and demands to know what is going on. Stella and Eunice distract Blanche with clothes and dressing. Blanche seems obsessed with the cleanliness of the grapes Eunice has brought, which is a metaphor for her own state of impurity. She refuses to walk past the men playing poker and waits which fits with Stella's need as she is waiting, too.

A doctor and nurse arrive, and Eunice announces that Blanche has visitors. The polka music plays and Blanche continues to believe it is Shep who is coming to take her away. As she passes by the poker table, the men, except for Mitch, stand awkwardly. Blanche is fearful when she sees the doctor and nurse instead of Shep. She goes back in, and Stanley asks her if she forgot something.

The lurid and sinuous shadows appear on the scrim again as the polka music builds to a crescendo. Stanley enters the room and Blanche screams and tries to run out. The matron speaks to Blanche and her voice echoes in a sinister manner to help the audience understand how Blanche is feeling. Stanley tears the paper lantern off the light and shines the bare bulb in Blanche's face; "she cries out as if the lantern were herself" (176) bringing the other men to their feet in the kitchen. The matron grabs Blanche and holds her as Mitch heads toward the bedroom. Stanley brushes past him on his way out; they get into a fight.

The doctor comes into the room and removes his hat. He crouches down and speaks softly to Blanche calling her "Miss Dubois." At Blanche's request, the doctor asks the nurse to let her go and Blanche cooperates saying, "I have always depended on the kindness of strangers" (178) as he leads her out of the house.

Echoing Stanley's cries in scene four, Stella calls out for her sister: "Blanche! Blanche! Blanche!" (178) as the doctor, the nurse and Blanche leave the scene. Eunice hands Stella her baby and Stanley soothes his crying wife. The men resume their poker game as if the entire play had never happened.

## Motifs

**Color:** The bright colors of scene three are repeated here indicating that things are returning to the way they were before Blanche's arrival.

**Music:** The polka music plays as Blanche leaves the bathroom indicating her fragile state of mind. The polka music also plays as Blanche sees the doctor and the nurse followed by drums followed by the polka all punctuated by the echoing calls of the nurse show Blanche's building panic and mental breakdown.

**Violence:** The writhing and grotesque shapes on the scrim remind the audience of Blanche's brutal rape by Stanley as the doctor and nurse arrive to take her to a mental hospital.

## Characterization
   ❖   Blanche: Blanche tries desperately to retain her dignity evoking Pathos as she is taken away, as though going out for the evening, by the doctor and his nurse.

46

❖ Stella: Stella has made her choice in her refusal to believe Blanche's "story" about being raped by Stanley. Although she is visibly upset by Blanche's removal, she is characterized as relieved that her life is going back to normal. Williams states in his stage directions, "there is something luxurious in her complete surrender to crying now that her sister is gone" (179) and her eager return to Stanley's lusty embrace.

❖ Stanley: Stanley continues in his harsh treatment of Blanche. He uses his sexuality to soothe Stella once Blanche is gone and his life resumes its former order. Stanley has won.

## Allegorical reading of characters

An allegory is a story in which characters represent ideas as well as themselves. In this play, one could argue that Blanche represents the largely passive and dying agrarian South that began its decline with the Civil War. Its values are old and fading, its institutions, like Belle Reve, are lost to modernity, and its founding realities, like Blanche's fading beauty, cannot withstand the bright light of modernity. One could argue that Stanley represents the active, new, industrial South filled with raw, powerful energies ready to take advantages of the weaknesses of the Old South for its advantage. Progress, depicted by Stanley Kowalski, moves ahead at all costs and is national in its pride. Stella is the meeting place where the Old South and the New South merge, the place where mediation is needed and where the new generation is born.

Ask yourself:

- Blanche's statement that she has "always depended on the kindness of strangers" (178) is highly ironic. What is the effect of this irony on your understanding of and feeling for Blanche? Is she a sympathetic character?

- What do you think of Stella as a character? Do you think she made the right choice in choosing not to believe Blanche? Is Stella a sympathetic character? What did Williams achieve in depicting Stella as he has?

- Stanley is a compelling character – a force. What do you think about him as a person? He is the antagonist of the play, but is he a villain? What did Williams achieve in his depiction of Stanley? Is Stanley dated as a character?

## Close Reading of a Text

Reading a work closely lies at the root of any good paper about the work. Once you have the background work suggested in Some Possible Angles for Analysis, you can start a close reading of the text. Close reading involves annotating or taking notes on a text. Post-it notes come in very handy for this task. I recommend having a variety of colors for this task.

### Step One:
Determine the **purpose**: Before reading any text, you should try to determine why you are reading it.

### Ask yourself:
- What is the assignment?
- What is the larger context of the text? Is it related to other texts?
- What kind of assessment do I expect?

Determine the **type of text** and think about text structure expectations. Each type of texts comes with a structure which we have learned as readers.

Ask yourself:
- How are plays structured?
- What do I need to bring to the reading of a play?
- What are the conventions of a play?

### Step Two

Spend a few seconds thinking about the topic to **activate prior knowledge**. One way our brain works is that we file like information together. By activating prior knowledge we are, in effect, opening a file folder in our brains.

Ask yourself: What do I know about Shakespeare and Elizabethan England? What do I know about the play Hamlet?

**Read actively** – with a pen/pencil in hand and a hi-lighter available.

Use a combination of brief **comments** in the margins.

- Questions
- Connections
- Comments
- Challenges
- Summarize

**Circle** words that you are unsure about and may need to look up or learn

**Underline or hi-light** – be careful not to over-do

Key points the writer is making
Special terms to discipline – e.g.
Literary devices

**Questioning/ challenging the text:**
- Why does the writer use this specific word?
- What does this mean? I don't get it?
- How does this allusion contribute to the meaning?
- Does the title help me understand meaning or tone?

## Step Three

Take notes as you read. I like to do motif traces. That means noticing motifs or recurring images in a text. For example, a motif in *A Streetcar Named Desire* is animal imagery. I would choose one color Post-it note for that theme and stick it next to every time Williams uses animal imagery with a note about its significance.

Another theme in in *A Streetcar Named Desire* violence. You can also take notes directly in the book, if you own it, using colored hi-lighters or you can set up some notebook pages for the motifs and take notes.

Animal Imagery

| Page#/ scene | Character | Passage | Significance |
|---|---|---|---|
| | | | |
| | | | |
| | | | |

Fantasy vs Reality

| Page# scene | character | Passage | Significance |
|---|---|---|---|
| | | | |
| | | | |
| | | | |

Light vs Dark

| Page# scene | character | Passage | Significance |
|---|---|---|---|
| | | | |
| | | | |
| | | | |

Step Four

Questioning a Text:   Note / challenge/ react to the author's use of language:

- the effect of diction and/or syntax on reading
- the effect of choices in speaker and/or point of view
- the effect of tone — especially irony
- the effect juxtaposition
- the effect figures of speech & stylistic devices

- the effect of repetition on reading/ types of repetition: word, phrase, action, pattern
- the effect pacing and the way the writer controls the speed with which we read a passage
- the narrative devices — action, sequence of events,
- the effect setting, characters, meaning, theme

Now that you have the book read, you can begin the brainstorming process.

# Possible Creative Writing Tasks

**Character Journal**

Assume the role or persona of a character whose perspective about the action is not explored in the work you are studying. You can take a bit of poetic license here and be creative.

For example, you could observe the action in *A Streetcar Named Desire* from Eunice's point of view. What would Eunice have to say if he were observing Hamlet from the beginning of the play? Or Mitch?

This choice works best if you choose a character who can be present through the entire work. Your entries should have a voice or sound like the character you are portraying and reveal some insight into the text you are exploring. A journal differs from a diary in that it allows the reader to make observations and reflection on those observation. They should offer more insight than emotion.

**Exchange of Letters**

Assume the person of two characters whose perspective about the action is not explored in the work you are studying. The letter writers can even be people outside of the text observing the action. Write a series of letters exchanged between these two characters in which they offer insight into the motivations and events unfolding in the work.

Your letters should have an appropriate degree of formality depending on the relationship. Your letters should follow the rules of letter writing: date, salutation, closing, signature.

**Missing Scene or Alternate Ending**

All works of literature have scenes that evoke curiosity in readers because they leave us wondering what happened. Select a scene that leaves you wondering and flesh it out. Make it fit seamlessly into the work as a whole. Your piece should imitate the style of the write and follow the conventions of the genre: novel, play, poem. It should also make sense given the entirety of the work.

An **alternate ending** works the same way and should fit seamlessly at the end of the work. For example, if you write an alternate ending for Romeo and Juliet where the couple survive and all ends happily, then your ending has to make sense. How would the play be different if Stella chose to believe Blanche's "story" of rape at Stanley's hand?

## TIP:

If you have been asked to or decided to write a missing scene or an alternate ending to a work of fiction, it is likely that you are going to be assessed on several things:

Understanding of the work read.
Understanding of genre conventions.
Writing skills.

Your piece of fiction should be grounded in the text you are exploring including the setting, the characters' personality traits, the surrounding plot events, motifs, themes, and the writer's style. Your piece needs to subtly reveal that you understand the work while you are offering fresh insight. In other words, you can be creative, BUT you have to stick to the story.

You need to include conventions of fiction such a characterization, plot and conflict, dialogue, and setting.

# Possible Essay Topics

Discuss the **ending of the work** under discussion. In what ways was the ending satisfying to you as a reader, and in what ways was the ending unsatisfying. Does the work leave you with more questions than answers? Is the work artistically flawed in the way it ends?

Playwrights often use setting, action, characterization, character interactions and dialogue to create atmosphere and/or to build tension. **Discuss the techniques** used by the playwright and their effect on the atmosphere and the audiences reaction to the events.

Select **a significant object** in the work you are exploring and discuss its significance and its contribution to meaning. The object should work both literally and symbolically.

**Morally Ambiguous or Evil Character:** Discuss an important character in the work who reveals himself or herself to be either evil or morally ambiguous (at times good and at times evil). Discuss the effect of the characters actions on the meaning of the text as a whole.

Discuss the significance of the **social and political context** in which the work was created and published and their impact on relevance and/or meaning.

Discuss a **character who is alienated** from the society in which he or she lives because of religion, race or culture. How does this character's alienation shed light on the values and belief systems of the times in which the work was written and contemporary values?

Discuss the **atmosphere** of a scene in the work and discuss how it reinforces setting and meaning/theme.

# Literary Criticism

Literary Criticism is an umbrella term for a variety of lenses through which we can examine a text whether the text is a play, a novel, a poem, a film, a comic strip, or a painting. There are many different theories or schools behind literary criticism. I will give you a brief overview of each. There are many books, journals and websites where you can expand your understanding of one of these theories should you wish.

Sometimes it is fun to adopt one of these lenses in order to examine a work.

Reader Response Theory

This is one of the most common theories used to explore literature throughout school. It is based on the concept that the role of the reader cannot be omitted from any discussion of a text, for the reader brings a lifetime of experience, opinions, and connections to any text creating an individual interpretation. In fact, readers actively engage with a text and create meaning. Much of the focus of literary analysis before reader response theory was on the author and historical context of a work.

Think about a cartoon film such as *Cars* that can be enjoyed by viewers of all ages. The film will have different meaning for different people based on their age and life experience. That is where the analysis comes in – looking at the different interpretive communities and their construction of meaning of a text on a personal level. One could look at specific images of a text, scenes, words, or tropes.

Employing this critical lens requires you as a reader to examine yourself as a reader, to explore the effectiveness of a text for readers such as yourself (an interpretive community), and support your conclusions with textual evidence.

Ask Yourself:

- How did I react to the text?
- Which life experiences led me to that reaction?
- What aspects of the text (words, images, action, characterization) caused this reaction?
- Is the text effective in conveying meaning for me? How?

Feminist Theory

Feminist Theory explores the way a text reinforces or subverts/ undermines the oppression of women economically, socially, psychologically or politically. By using this lens, one can shift the focus away from a male dominated view and examine perspectives and experiences of women, gender inequalities and differences, gender oppression, and institutions that foster oppression.

This theory developed in several waves over the past several hundred years. The goal of feminism is social awareness and change.

First Wave Feminist refers to those early feminists and suffragettes who were among the first to rally against sexual inequality. Mary Wollstonecraft wrote *A Vindication of the Rights of Women* in 1792 pointing out gender inequalities of British women. In the United States women fought and won the right to vote in 1920.

Second Wave Feminism refers to the 1950s and 1960s when the Women's Rights Movement was prevalent and feminist organizations such as NOW (National Organization of Women) formed to advocate for equal rights in the workplace, sexual and reproductive rights, and property rights. Second Wave feminism also brought domestic abuse, sexual abuse and rape concerns to the forefront allowing for social discourse and eventual and gradual change.

Third Wave is the current feminist movement which began in the 1990s, many say with Anita Hill and her charges of sexual harassment against Supreme Court Judge Clarence Thomas. Her struggle brought the prevalence of sexual harassment and workplace sexism and abuses to the forefront.

Fourth Wave began in 2012 and is rooted in the idea that all humans are equal and focuses on all marginalized groups seeking equal pay and opportunity, social mobility and freedom to make choice about one's own body. There is a goal to call out those who abuse power and oppress others.

Some terms

| | |
|---|---|
| Patriarchy | a term to define a social system which is male lead and those who hold power are primarily male leading to a system which supports and promotes male interests in order to retain hegemony or dominance of men to the exclusion and oppression of others. |
| Misogyny | a term used to discuss an apparent attitude of hatred or distrust toward women based solely on their gender. It manifests in sexual violence toward women, hate speech, sexual objectification, hostility and gender discrimination. |
| Marginalization | term used to describe the system efforts of those in power to oppress and keep those without power, voiceless, and/or underprivileged. |
| Gender | a term currently used to describe one's identification with a place on the spectrum between masculine and feminine. While sex describes physical characteristics at birth, gender describes ones identification as either masculine, feminine, both or neither. |
| Gender Identity | – a term used to describe the deeply personal and internal sense or understanding a person has of their gendered self: masculine, feminine or other. |

| | Here are a few types of gender identity: <br><br> • agender – someone who identifies as being without a gender or gender free <br> • genderfluid – someone whose gender identity changes on the gender spectrum <br> • non-binary – someone who identifies as neither male or female also called gender queer <br> • transgender – a term used to describe and individual who identifies with a gender other than the sex one was born into. Some transgender individuals use a combination of hormone therapies and surgery to alter their birth sex to the gender with which they identify such as Bruce Jenner becoming Caitlyn Jenner. |
|---|---|
| Intersectionality | a term coined by Rebecca Walker to describe the layers of oppression faced by women: gender, class, race, sexual orientation, disability, etc. |

Ask Yourself:
- What are the power dynamic between men and women in this text? Does one sex have more power than the other?
- How are male and female roles defined?
- What is masculine and what is feminine?
- Do characters in the play assume different genders and for what purpose?
- What does this text say about building a female group/sisterhood to resist male authority?

Postcolonial Theory

Postcolonial theory examines the voices of those cultures that were once held by colonial powers and the impact of colonization on culture such as power structures, religion, politics and economics. Historically, Europeans or those in power wrote the history and controlled the discourse about the colonized, but Postcolonial theory examines the destructive impact of European hegemony on subjugated cultures.

*Orientalism* by Edward Said is an import book for studying Postcolonial theory. Here is an overview of the basics of the book. One of the main concepts is that West has set up a tension with the East between extreme opposites through its depiction of the orient in art and literature.

Attributes of Occident and Orient are in binary opposition.

| The West | The Orient |
|---|---|
| Rational | Sensual |
| Industrious | Lazy |
| Civilized | Savage |
| Monogamous | Bigamist |
| Sophisticated | Simple |
| Changes Over Time | |
| 18th C    corrupted | 18th C Pure and noble |
| 18th C Biologically superior | 18th C biologically inferior |
| 19th C    discoverer | 19th C discovered |
| 20th C  seek peace | 20th C  violent |
| 20th C  benevolent | 20th C  cruel |
| 20th C  order | 20th C  chaos |

The book is organized chronologically beginning with 18th century boom in writing of all genres. The last quarter of the book is about modernity and the Orientalization of the Arab.

**Key points:**
- ✓ The East was Orientalized not only because it was discovered by Europeans to be Oriental but because it submitted or allowed itself to be Orientalized.
- ✓ Europeans created domestic images of the Orient in an effort to control what was feared and misunderstood. In 18th and 19th

century art the Oriental was often depicted in paintings as sensual, lazy, feminine, and passive.
✓ Western thought systems lean toward classification into types and binaries thus giving the West authority to rule

Looking at the world through *Orientalism* destabilizes the Grand Narrative of the West or the stories we tell ourselves to justify our civilization by giving voice to the oppressed and destabilizing key assumptions. One assumption of the Grand Narrative of Colonialism was that Colonist were bringing civilization (i.e. government, religion, education) to those who had none. This assumption nullifies any religious, political or cultural attributes of the colonized and implies that they need saving. Orientalism also place a focus on hybridity or the intersection of culture rather than the devaluing of one culture over another.

Some terms

| otherness | a term which describes that part of the self (Dominant Culture) which is an alter ego or at times a threat or which cannot be understood and as a result feared or that which must be dominated or subsumed |
|---|---|
| Hybridity | that which comes into being through the intersection of self and other – colonizer and colonized, occident and orient, dominant culture and counter culture |
| White Man's Burden | the idea that white Westerners believed they are destined to rule non-whites based on a poem by Rudyard Kipling |
| Subaltern | A term used by Said to describe those outside the power structure of the Dominant Culture; the marginalized. |

Ask Yourself:
• How does this text represent cultural differences in shaping the world in which we and the characters live?

- What group does the text identify as other or strange and how are they treated?
- Can the text be read as an allegory for colonialism if it is not overtly about colonialism?

Marxist Theory

This school of criticism is based on the works of Karl Marx and the impact of a socio-economic system on a people or individual. The main question to be explored in Marxist theory is "Who does the work and who benefits from that work?" It also looks at class systems and their impact on the individual. The theory is rooted in the doctrine that a revolution led by the working class will come in which Capitalism will be abolished and all wealth and social responsibility will be shared equally.

Ask Yourself:
- Does the text support the ideology of the upper class to the detriment of the lower classes?
- What values does the text champion or subvert?
- Do characters from different classes interact and what is the result of that interaction?
- What class is the author and what class does the text benefit?

Literary Darwinism

Literary Darwinism is a school of critical theory that looks at works of literature through the lens of Charles Darwin and his theories of evolution as well as many interesting off-shoots such as evolutionary psychology and behavioral genetics. Literary Darwinism is a complex theoretical structure but the basics include an examination of a range of human motivations and behaviors in relation to genetically transmitted traits and their intersection with culture. Basic human needs such as survival, reproduction, the acquisition of resources such as food, shelter, wealth, a living in a social are elements to be examined as universally human behaviors. For example in the works of Jane Austin, the women compete to win high-status and wealthy men while the men compete to win the most beautiful women.

Natural selection (survival of the fittest) According to an article in the New York Times by D.T. Max, Mrs. Bennett's obsession to marry of her daughters in Pride and Prejudice is her deeply ingrained or "hardwired" need to transmit her genetic material to subsequent generations.

- ❖ Looks at humanity adapted and survived through storytelling
- ❖ Readers relate to fictional characters because they are social active and the conflicts of characters because they reflect hardwired impulse to compete for resources
- ❖ Storytelling is a universally human that captures evolutionary behaviors, social engagements which gave our ancestors an advantage by allowing them to practice a variety of situations

Warning: Literary Darwinism is not without its critics because many Literary Darwinists express a hostility towards humanities in favor of science; however, it can be a fun and interesting lens through which to look at literature.

Ask yourself:
- Does the work have something to say about evolution? Survival of the fittest?

Works Cited

Max, D.T. "The Literary Darwinists." *The New York Times.* 6 November 2005. Web. 9 February 2019.

Queer Theory

As a critical lens through which one can study literature, Queer Theory has its roots in Women and Gender studies. Queer, the previously pejorative word for homosexual, has been co-opted by the movement which fights against societal expectations that heterosexuality is normal. Queer in this context means gender expressions outside binary male/female or out of the ordinary. Theory is interested in exploring and smashing neat categories of gender.

The function of Queer Theory like Feminist Theory and Postcolonial Theory is to examine power struggles and marginalization related to gender. Queer Theory explores the ways gender and sexuality is discussed and see gender as a spectrum rather than a binary of male and female. Anxiety about gender and homophobia arise, one could argue, from the rigid gender expectations of the past; true understanding of one's gender and relationships comes from understanding of all genders and their relationships.

Our understanding of gender has deepened as a result of the work of critical theorist and social reformers. We live in a time when most people recognized that gender and the sex a person is born with are not fixed thanks to the celebrity transgendering of Bruce/Caitlyn Jenner, Laverne Cox of Orange is the New Black , and Chelsea Manning to name a few. News headlines often focus on transgender issues and rights that did not exist twenty years ago such as transgender rest rooms in schools, transgender military personnel, and discrimination against transgenders. As a result of social issues around gender, it seem logical that we would begin to look at literary works in terms of conforming or nonconforming to gender expectations and whether or not gender expectations are a reality.

Some terms

| Heteronomativity | The theory that humans fall into distinct and compulsory gender roles that are both opposing and complimentary: male and female and that people fulfill the expected |
| --- | --- |

| | social roles of those genders. The terms also means that heterosexuality is the normal sexuality. |
|---|---|
| Gender as performance | Judith Butler, in her book Gender Trouble, argues that gender rather than being entirely biological is a complex reality of that which is acted out or performed as reality. Performance in this context does not imply a role but rather the repetition of behavior that builds a gender reality. |
| Androgyny | Having characteristics of both female and male |
| Bigender | A tendency to identify with one gender or the other either simultaneously or under different circumstances or at different times |
| Binary | A division of gender into two opposing and mutually exclusive categories of male and female |
| Cross gender | Adopting the mannerisms or clothing of the opposite sex; often used for those who are transgendered but have not gone through the physical process yet. |
| Gender queer | Umbrella term for those who don't identify with tradition gender binaries: male or female. For example, a gender queer person may identify as both male and female or neither male of female, something other than male of female. |
| Intersectionality | The idea that gender identity intersect and that race, ethnicity, gender, language, education and class all intersect to create a complex and often cumulative system of oppression. |

Ask Yourself:
- How do elements of the text such as character and image support the traditional binary roles of gender?
- What elements of the text are outside the traditional gender roles of male and female?

- What are the effects of these elements on meaning or experience?
- What elements of the text question or subvert traditional gender roles of male and female and what do they tell us?
- What elements are in the middle or exhibit both genders?
- How does work explore or illustrate sexual identity and/or sexuality?
- Does the sexuality and sexual identities fall within or outside the traditional male/female binary or heterosexual?
- Does the author appear in the work in drag or as a different gender?
- Does the author's gender and experiences related to gender appear in the work and to what effect?

# Literary Terms Related to Fiction

If you took your phone to a repair man and he referred to parts as thing-a-ma-jigs or do-hickies you would not have a very good impression of his or her abilities. You expect people to use the terms connected to their trade. The same goes with writing about literature: your reader expects you to use some common terms that literate people know. Here is a list of some terms you may find useful.

## Greek Drama: Tragedy

The ideas below are expressed in a text called *Poetics* by the philosopher and critic Aristotle in which he details the attributes of a perfect tragedy. It may be interesting to look at the play through this lens.

**Artistic Unity**: That condition of a successful literary work whereby all its elements work together to achieve its central purpose. Nothing is included that is irrelevant to central purpose; nor is anything excluded that is essential to central purpose.

**Catharsis:** a term used by Aristotle to describe some sort of emotional release experienced by the audience at the end of a successful tragedy. In *Poetics*, Aristotle sees the objective of tragedy as catharsis -- the purgation of tension aroused through pity and fear. The Greek term is ambiguous and was not explained by Aristotle. Some possible interpretations:

1) the spectator, through vicarious participation, learns through the experience of the protagonist to avoid pity and fear

2) the spectator has pity and fear aroused in human connection with the protagonist and internal agitations are vicariously relieved while viewing tragedy

3) the tragic hero is a scapegoat on which the excessive emotions of the spectator can be placed, leaving the spectator calm at the end

**Catastrophe**: the conclusion of a play, particularly a tragedy, the final stage in the falling action ending the dramatic conflict and ending the plot. This term has been replaced in modern drama tragedies with the term denouement.

**Deus ex Machina** (god from the machine) The resolution of a plot by use of a highly improbable chance or coincidence (so named from the practice of some Greek dramatists of having a god descend from heaven at the last possible minute -- in the theater by means of machines -- to rescue the protagonist from an impossible situation)

*Hamartia:* The error, frailty, mistaken judgment, or misstep through which the fortunes of the hero of a tragedy are reversed. Hamartia is not a flaw in a character, although sometimes hamartia is erroneous called a tragic flaw. Hamartia can be an unwitting, even a necessary, misstep in "doing" rather than an error in character. Hamartia can be the result of bad judgment, bad character, ignorance, inherited, weakness, accident, any action or failure to perform any action.

**Recognition:** the moment in a story when previously unknown or withheld information is revealed to the protagonist, resulting in the discovery of the truth of his or her situation and, usually, a decisive change in course for that character

**Reversal of fortune:** According to Aristotle, the reversal of fortune is a movement from happiness to misery in the protagonist.

**Tragedy:** A type of drama, opposed to comedy, which depicts the causally related events that lead to the downfall and suffering of the protagonist, a person of unusual moral or intellectual stature or outstanding abilities.

**Tragic flaw:** an error or defect in the tragic hero that leads to his or her downfall, such as greed, pride, or ambition. In literary circles in the past, it was popular to attribute the downfall of a tragic hero to a flaw, an error, or a defect which contributes to his or her downfall. Modern criticism argues that the "flaw" is an integral and even defining part of the hero's character. Oedipus's thirst for knowledge and Antigone's devotion to duty are hardly flaws; rather these qualities are at the heart of the hero's character.

**Tragic hero:** a person of high status or of great importance who: is neither entirely good, nor entirely bad experiences a reversal fortune due to a mistake or a character flaw and whose suffering is out of proportion to deed

## Other Drama Terms:

**Aside:** the character in a play turns to the audience and speaks directly to them. It is accepted that the other characters on the stage do not "hear" the comments.

**Foil:** a character in a work whose behavior and values contrast with those of another character in order to highlight the distinctive temperament of that character (usually the protagonist). In Macbeth, Mac Duff acts as a foil to Macbeth because he is an honest and honorable man.

**Soliloquy:** the character in a play is alone on the stage revealing his or her innermost thoughts and feelings.

## Elements of Plot

**Plot:** a series of related events that make up a story, a novel, a play, or a script. Here is a breakdown of the various parts of a plot.

**Exposition**: the information we need to understand the story including the setting the main character, and his or her problem

**Rising Action**: those conflicts and complications which build tension and suspense

**Conflict:** the struggle or clash between opposing characters, forces, or emotions. You may have learned these types of conflict: person versus self; person versus person; person versus nature; person versus society; person versus fate. Stories often include multiple conflicts.

**Complications:** a series of conflict related problems that the character has to deal with that increase tension building to the climax of the story. For example, a young woman has become lost in a blizzard (conflict: person versus nature). As she is stumbling about in the blinding snow looking for more firewood, her shelter collapses burying her supplies under a huge mound of snow and ice (complication).

**Suspense:** a feeling of tension or anxiety we feel in a story when we wonder what will happen next. Suspense is created through setting, conflict, complication, pacing, mood and atmosphere.

**Climax**: the most exciting or tense moment of the story when something happens that will determine the outcome of the conflict.

**Falling Action**: those events which occur after the climax and which contribute to the resolution/dénouement.

**Resolution:** the part of the plot where the conflict is resolved.

**Dénouement**: a French word that means "the unraveling of the knot" created by conflict and suspense; the resolution.

**Foreshadowing**: the writer provides hints about what will happen in the future contributing to tension and atmosphere.

## Diction

Diction is a fancy word that means word choice. Diction is a simple idea because we choose our words whenever we write or speak. That's why writing about diction can be a bit tricky.

**TIP**: Always use an adjective before the word diction!

Words that describe diction:

| | |
|---|---|
| cacophonous | words that have a harsh, grating sound |
| concrete | words that are specific and create vivid images |
| concise | words that are specific and direct; to the point |
| connotative | words that carry emotional or cultural meaning beyond the dictionary definition |
| detached | words that create a sense of isolation and separateness |
| euphonious | words that create a pleasant sound |
| formal | academic or elevated words |
| Informal | casual, relaxed |
| Pedantic | scholarly; didactic (lecturing) |

## Tone

Tone is the speaker or writer's attitude toward the subject matter. Tone is achieved through many elements of a piece including diction, syntax, connotation, figurative language and stylistic choices made by the writer. Detecting tone helps the reader understand the purpose and meaning of a work. In long works of fiction, tone may shift between scenes: however, so works may have a sustained tone – often satiric or ironic.

TIP: If you want to write about the feeling that a work evokes in the reader, go to the section on mood or atmosphere.

Here are some words to describe tones:

Neutral Tone words

| candid/sincere | honest and impartial |
| contemplative | deeply thoughtful |
| detached | disinterested; aloof |
| didactic | instructive; lecturing |
| informative | unbiased/ to convey information |

Positive Tone Words

| amused | pleasurably entertained or diverted |
| authoritative | substantiated by authority/ expertise |
| enthusiastic | vehement; ardent |
| playful | pleasantly humorous or jesting |
| reverent | deeply respectful |
| sympathetic | understanding the feelings of another |
| whimsical | excessively playful; capricious |

Sad Tone Words

| Elegiac | looking at the past with mournful longing |
| Melancholy | gloomy state of mind; sorrowfully |
| Nostalgic | expressing a desire to return to the past |
| sentimental | excessively emotional |

Tone words to describe a speaker with an agenda

| Bitter | hostile; harshly disagreeable |
| Callous | insensitive; indifferent; unsympathetic |
| choleric | extremely easily angered and bitter |
| condescending | regarding audience with contempt |
| critical | inclined to find fault with; judgmental |
| cynical | distrusting the motives of others |

| obsequious | showing extreme deference |

## Humor-Irony-Sarcasm-Satire

| caustic | bitter; severely critical and/or sarcastic |
|---|---|
| contemptuous | judging that which is observed as worthless |
| facetious | not meant to be taken seriously or literally |
| ironic | what is expected is not what is received |
| irreverent | showing a lack of respect |
| mocking | to treat with contempt or ridicule |

## Atmosphere and Mood

The literary terms atmosphere and mood describe the emotions of a reader or viewer when experiencing a piece of literature. The author creates a mood through his use of specific diction, one, figurative language such as symbolism, allusion, and metaphor to evoke emotions in the reader in the same way that film-makers use lighting, camera angle and sound effects to create a mood such as frightful, suspenseful, or joyful.

## Irony

Irony is an effect of a writer's choices on the reader. Irony occurs when there is a difference between what we expect and what we get. What we expect as readers/viewers is a complex outgrowth of our culture and our experiences. When our expectations are manipulated by a writer the impact is irony.

Three Basic Types of Irony:

- Verbal irony occurs when the speaker says one thing but means another thing.

- Situational irony occurs when we are led to expect one thing to happen, but another thing happens.
- Dramatic irony occurs when the reader/audience knows something important that a main character does not know.

# Brainstorming Before Writing

Most of the work involved in writing goes on before you sit down at the keyboard. First, you need to come up with some ideas about your topic. You need to brainstorm. Here are some common brainstorming methods other than webbing.

**Thinking Like a Journalist**: 5w's and H  who? what? when? where? why? how?

**Cubing**: 6 perspectives
- describe — what is it?
- compare — what is it similar to? different from?
- analyze — what are its parts? what is it made of?
- association — what does it make you think of?
- apply — how can it be used
- argue — how can you make a case for or against?

**3 perspectives**
- describe it in detail
- trace the history
- connect it to other topics and ideas

**A - Z**    think of something about your topic for every letter of the alphabet

# Some tips to improve your writing!

## Use Literary Present Tense

When we write about literature and art, one of the conventions or rules of etiquette is to use literary present tense. In other words, we write about the piece as it is occurring right now — even if it was written in the past — because we are experiencing it right now.

We often write about writer/poet/author's use of language and devices to create a certain effect (see chapter Writing about Literature). Again, we write as if the work/author is alive. The use of literary present tense helps avoid awkward construction.

*How do I write in literary present tense?*

Use active verbs in present tense to describe what the writer is doing. Some active verbs to in signal phrases or introductory phrases for quotations. See the chart on the next page for some ideas.

| Writer is Neutral | | Writer Suggests/Predicts | |
|---|---|---|---|
| comments | mentions | speculates | |
| records | states | asks | |
| describes | notes | assesses | |
| relates | points out | concludes | |
| explains | observes | finds | |
| thinks | shows | predicts | |
| illustrates | | | |
| writes | | | |
| Writer is persuading | | Writer is analyzing | |
| believes | hypothesizes | explores | examines |
| maintains | supports | dissects | sorts |
| proposes    holds | contends | breaks down | |
| suggests | claims | investigates | |
| defends | insists | separates | |

| Writer agrees with | Writer disparages | |
|---|---|---|
| concurs | condemns | laments |
| concedes | derides | bemoans |
| admits | complains | deprecates |
| accepts | deplores | |

## Avoid Passive Voice

Passive voice a construction that focusses on the receiver of an action rather than the doer of an action. Developing writers often fall into a pattern of using passive voice in an attempt to avoid using "I" in their pieces or in an attempt to build a sense of distance or authority.

Here are some examples of sentence about literature written in passive voice:

- EX: *A Streetcar Named Desire* was written by Tennessee Williams.
- FIX: Tennessee Williams wrote *A Streetcar Named Desire.*

- EX: Stella was smacked on the butt by Stanley.
- FIX: Stanley playfully smacked Stella on the butt.

- EX: The plate was thrown across the room.
- FIX: Stanley threw a plate across the room.

In some cases, if you want to emphasize a characters passivity, you can use passive voice.

- EX: Stella finds himself unable to resist Stanley's raw sexuality.

## Correctly Integrating Your Quotations

Quoted material and summarized or paraphrased material are used to support a writer's ideas. Beginning writers often try to use quotations as ideas instead of as support. Here are some guidelines for using quotations:

*Avoid using quotations in your introduction, thesis or in topic sentences.*

Example of the wrong way to use quotations: as a body paragraph topic sentence:

The article "The Beast in Lord of the Flies" states, "the beast epitomizes evil; however, does it represent the potential evil in the hearts of every human, or does the beast embody an external force of evil or savagery that is held in check by rules and civilization?" (par. 2)

*solution*: Use the quotation to support your topic sentence

The symbolism of the Beast in *Lord of the Flies* is complex and cannot be categorized simply as a representation of the evil and darkness within, for the depths of the human psyche are a complex interaction of impulses and motivations. The article "The Beast in Lord of the Flies" explores the symbolism of the beast raising some interesting questions while stating that the beast does symbolize: "The beast epitomizes evil; however, does it represent the potential evil in the hearts of every human, or does the beast embody an external force of evil or savagery that is held in check by rules and civilization?" (par. 2)

NEVER have a quotation in your paper that is not attached to your words. Avoid sentences where the quotation comes first followed by your words.

How not to use a quotation:

The symbolism of the Beast in *Lord of the Flies* is complex and cannot be categorized simply as a representation of the evil and darkness within, for the depths of the human psyche are a complex interaction of impulses and motivations. **"The beast epitomizes evil; however, does it represent the potential evil in the hearts of every human, or does the beast embody an external tendency to evil or savagery that is held in check by rules and civilization?"** **("The Beast in *Lord of the Flies*").** This quotation shows that the human psyche is complex and the symbolism is complex, too.

*solution:* Introduce the quoted material with words of your own including an action verb "explores" and "raising some insightful questions" and "stating." This allows you to establish a context and purpose or analysis of the quotation:

The symbolism of the Beast in *Lord of the Flies* is complex and cannot be categorized simply as a representation of the evil and darkness within, for the depths of the human psyche are a complex interaction of impulses and motivations. **"The Beast in *Lord of the Flies*" explores the symbolism of the beast raising some insightful questions while stating that the beast does symbolize "evil; however, does it represent the potential evil in the hearts of every human, or does the beast embody an external tendency to evil or savagery that is held in check by rules and civilization?" (par. 2)**

## Punctuating your quotations 3 simple ways!

#1 with a colon : Ask yourself: Can the phrase before the quotation stand on its own as a sentence? If the answer is "yes," use a colon.

EX: In her novel *Northanger Abbey*, Jane Austin immediately establishes an ironic tone when describing her heroine Catherine Morland: No one who had ever seen Catherine Morland in her infancy would have supposed her to be a heroine (1).

#2 with a comma , Ask yourself: Can the phrase before the quotation stand on its own as a sentence? If the answer is "no," use a comma.

EX: Jane Austin further describes Catherine as having, "a thin, awkward figure, a sallow skin without color, dark lank hair, and strong features" (1).

#3 no punctuation -- a quotation nugget Ask yourself: if I take away the quotation marks, would I need any punctuation? If the answer is "no," don't use punctuation BUT do use quotation marks.

EX: In addition to describing her heroine as unattractive, Austin describes her as "occasionally stupid" (2).

# Transitional and Linking Words

Transitions are important because they help your reader follow your thoughts — use them!

| Show Location | | Show time | |
|---|---|---|---|
| above | around | meanwhile | First |
| beneath | down | then | later |
| near | away from | next | second |
| behind | inside | after | afterward |

| | | | |
|---|---|---|---|
| across | in front of | today | third |
| beside | in front of | at | immediately |
| outside | in back of | tomorrow | until |
| below | among | when | finally |
| against | under | before | |
| beyond | between | yesterday | |
| over | into | as soon as | |
| through | | during | |
| | | soon | |

| Show Similarities/Compare | | Show Differences / Contrast | |
|---|---|---|---|
| in the same | likewise | but | however |
| way | also | yet | although |
| like | | on the other hand | even though |
| similarly | | | otherwise |
| as | | | still |

| Emphasize a Point | | Conclude or Summarize | |
|---|---|---|---|
| again | for this reason | as a result | all in all |
| to emphasize | in fact | last | to sum up |
| above all | more | in summary | finally |
| to repeat | importantly | therefore | in conclusion |
| truly | | | |

| To add information | | To introduce an idea |
|---|---|---|
| again | additionally | for example |
| and | moreover | notably |
| for example | in addition | to illustrate |
| furthermore | next | for instance |
| also | likewise | including |
| besides | another | such as |
| for instance | equally important | |
| finally | | |

# The 5-Paragraph Essay about Literature

The 5-paragraph essay is a standard essay framework that is taught as an organizing tool for developing high school and college writers. It is ONE way of writing a paper; it is not the only way to write a paper. Once this format is mastered, it is a good practice to move on to a less formulaic style of paper writing.

As the writer of the paper, it is your job to make your ideas clear and convey them to the reader. It is NOT your reader's job to fill in places where ideas are missing or to guess what you are thinking. Make your ideas clear using active verbs and by keeping the author and his or her craft and the effectiveness of this craft as the topic of your paper rather than the poem or the story.

## Thesis

The thesis of your paper is the controlling idea or what you have say about the topic. A three-part thesis works very well organizing our paper because you will devote a paragraph to each part of your thesis.

Every sentence of your paper will relate to the thesis by

- supporting your ideas with direct quotations from the/a text.
- developing your idea by providing details and example
- acknowledging possible opposing view points
- comparing and contrasting ideas
- connecting to life or another piece of literature or popular culture

**Examples of three-part thesis:**
Williams uses the contrasting dualities of upper-class versus lower-class, fantasy versus reality, and light versus dark to create and build tension illuminating the theme that one must leave fantasy behind and face the real world with open eyes in order to thrive and survive.

Williams uses the contrasting dualities of fantasy and reality to stress the idea that one needs to leave fantasy behind and face reality in order to succeed through his characterization of Blanche, his characterization of Stanley and his use of the paper lantern as a symbol.

Williams guides audience reaction to staged events with blues piano and polka music, two very contrasting styles creating tension and heightening mood and atmosphere.

Williams explores new class structures in the New South through his characterization of Blanche, Stanley and Stella.

**Examples of Idea based thesis related to Literary Theory:**

Williams explores survival of the fittest in the new South by depicting Stanley Kowalski as a victorious, ruthless and at times savage man who defeats his enemy Blanche saving his lifestyle and family.

Williams creates irony when the hyper-male Stanley Kowalski serves as an avenger for the death of Blanche's spurned and suicidal homosexual husband by destroying Blanche.

Stanley Kowalski, a firm realist and a man who feels morally superior, functions as a superego enforcing his moral stance onto Blanche who lives in the guilt and delusions of her id.
**Thesis for essay about A Streetcar Named Desire:** Williams creates heartbreaking irony in his depiction of Blanche, a pathetic and tragic figure shattered in the transition from her Romantic girlhood and destined to roam searching for kindness, safety, and love.

**Body Paragraphs** – A paragraph is a group of related sentences. Each sentence in your paragraph is related to the specific part of the thesis you are exploring. Each body paragraph should have at least 6-7 sentences. Each body paragraph has a topic sentence: a specific sentence that states the topic of your paragraph.

Sample Topic sentence

Blanche came to stay with Stella as a last resort. She had no money and no one else to ask for help since she could not build any lasting relationships; however, she was not treated kindly by Stella and her husband.

Other things to include in a body paragraph:

- Definition of terms

- Supporting details – direct quotation from text (correctly embedded and cited) and analysis of the quotation. DO NOT say "this quotation means" – ever! The subject of each sentence should be the author or his choices.

- Discussion/ analysis – effectiveness of device in conveying meaning or in enhancing the reader's experience of the piece of writing under discussion.

- Examples or connections to everyday life

- Segue or transition sentence – a sentence crafted to move the reader from one paragraph to the next.

  Example: In addition to vivid imagery, Shakespeare uses connotative words to create atmosphere.

Sample body paragraph:

Blanche, we learn as the play unfolds, suffers from trauma after her young husband, whom she adored, shot himself; her entire existence subsequently has been an attempt to find shelter in a treacherous world where words can cause death. Filled with self-loathing and guilt, blaming herself for her thoughtless and cruel words to Allan about his homosexuality. The young Blanche had Romantic ideas about love and thought her young husband was "almost too fine to be human" (124). Yet, after she discovers him in the arms of a male lover, she responds with cruel words, "you disgust me" (115); Allan shoots himself a few moments later leading Blanche to believe she caused his death. As a literature teacher, Blanche appreciates the power of words: to inspire love, to make us more human, and to injure. Ironically, It is the brutish Stanley who uses cruel words under the guise of truth that completes Blanche's search for safety. Ironically, the hyper-male Stanley, destroys Blanche who destroyed the gentle, homosexual Allan. Ironically, Stanley's cruelty sends Blanche to the safest place – a mental hospital where she can indulge in her fantasies and escape the harsh, cruel world.

**Introduction**: Even though the introduction is the first paragraph your reader will see, I like to write my introduction last. After all, I want to make a good impression as a writer and to do that I need to be certain about my thoughts. The introduction has several purposes:

- Grab the attention/ interest of your reader
- Establish the work you are discussing and place it in a context: time, place, theme, etc.
- State your thesis as the last sentence of the introduction

**Parts of the introduction**
Hook or grab your readers attention or as the fishing metaphor implies "hook" her so you can reel her in. There are several ways to create a hook:

definition
rhetorical question
quotation from a work outside the text
thought provoking statement
short and pointed personal statement

Title and author of the piece

✓ A note about author names: In the body of the essay, you will refer to the author by his or her LAST name only. You are **not** an intimate friend of the writer and will not refer to him by his first name. William Shakespeare is NOT Will or William or Bill; he is Shakespeare.

✓ Titles of short stories, songs and poems are in "quotation marks" while book length works and films are in *italics* when typed or underlined when hand written.

✓ Context   When was the poem written?
            Why is it relevant now?
            Why are we reading it? (theme)

Sample Introduction

 Tennessee William writes his plays from his life experiences. Mental illness and homosexuality are two aspects of his life present in *A Streetcar Named Desire*. This rich play has shaped the way we look at class conflict in post WWII America with the hyper-macho Stanley Kowalski in his wife-beater t-shirt calling for his wife Stella and the fragile and broke southern belle Blanche who drinks too much and is a bit mad. We have hard working and hard playing men in bowling alleys and seated around a poker table masters of their home. However, it is Williams' characterization of Blanche that elicits the most powerful emotional response in the play. Williams creates heartbreaking irony in his depiction of Blanche, a pathetic and tragic figure shattered in the transition from her Romantic girlhood and destined to roam searching for kindness, safety, and love.

# Sample Essay

### The Tragic Irony of Blanche Dubois

Tennessee William writes his plays from his life experiences. Mental illness and homosexuality are two aspects of his life present in *A Streetcar Named Desire*. This rich play has shaped the way we look at class conflict in post WWII America with the hyper-macho Stanley Kowalski in his wife-beater t-shirt calling for his wife Stella and the fragile and broke southern belle Blanche who drinks too much and is a bit mad. We have hard working and hard playing men in bowling alleys and seated around a poker table masters of their home. However, it is Williams' characterization of Blanche that elicits the most powerful emotional response in the play. Williams creates heartbreaking irony in his depiction of Blanche, a pathetic and tragic figure shattered in the transition from her Romantic girlhood and destined to roam searching for kindness, safety, and love.

Blanche, we learn as the play unfolds, suffers from trauma after her young husband, whom she adored, shot himself; her entire existence subsequently has been an attempt to find shelter in a treacherous world where words can cause death. Filled with self-loathing and guilt, blaming herself for her thoughtless and cruel words to Allan about his homosexuality. The young Blanche had Romantic ideas about love and thought her young husband was "almost too fine to be human" (124). Yet, after she discovers him in the arms of a male lover, she responds with cruel words, "you disgust me" (115); Allan shoots himself a few moments later leading Blanche to believe she caused his death. As a literature teacher, Blanche appreciates the power of words: to inspire love, to make us more human, and to injure. Ironically, It is the brutish Stanley who uses cruel words under the guise of truth that completes Blanche's search for safety. Ironically, the hyper-male Stanley, destroys Blanche who destroyed the gentle, homosexual Allan. Ironically, Stanley's cruelty sends Blanche to the safest place – a mental hospital where she can indulge in her fantasies and escape the harsh, cruel world.

As a blossoming and Romantic woman, Blanche fell in love with a handsome, gentle young man who wrote poetry and made no physical demands. Tragically, she felt she let Allan down even on their honeymoon when she knew that she "failed him in some mysterious way" and wasn't able to "give him the help he needed but couldn't speak of" (114). When Allan commits suicide, Blanche is left with guilt and a warped new vision of love. She confesses she uses "intimacies with strangers" (146) to fill the empty void in her heart. To feel alive, Blanche seeks meaningless physical intimacy. Blanche falls back on her fantasy world of old-fashioned gentility when the cruelty of the world becomes more than she can bear. In contrast, Blanche uses her promiscuity and her ability to create fantasy for her lovers to survive in the world. She tells Mitch, "I don't tell the truth, I tell what ought to be the truth! And if that is sinful, then let me be damned for it!" (145) Ironically, it her lonely quest for love in the arms of strangers that earned Mitch's loathing and hatred and has ostracized her from her home in Laurel.

One of the most poignant lines in the play comes as Blanche is being taken to the mental hospital. The doctor, intervening to stop the nurse from manhandling Blanche, behaves like a gentleman, speaks to her softly, and addresses her a Miss Dubois. Blanche thanks him and says, "I have always depended on the kindness of strangers" (178). As we know, Blanche's life has been a string of gentleman whom she dated a few times and who, it is implied, gave her gifts and perhaps money to sustain herself, so her words are true; however, they are highly ironic. Blanche came to stay with Stella as a last resort. She had no money and no one else to ask for help since she could not build any lasting relationships; however, she was not treated kindly by Stella and her husband. She was tolerated at best. Stella, although she understood her sisters mental illness better than anyone else, chose to believe Stanley over Blanche when Blanche accused him of sexually assaulting her. Stella had a newborn and was in no position to leave Stanley and so, ironically, Blanche is taken away to a mental hospital where she will be totally dependent upon the kindness of strangers.

*A Streetcar Named Desire* is a complex play that builds tensions with dueling opposites such as light and dark, love and lust, and fantasy and reality. One effect of these dualities is a pervading irony that enhances his characterization of Blanche as a sad, lonely and pathetic woman suffering from post-traumatic stress disorder in a world that had no understanding of mental illness.

Work Cited

Williams, Tennessee. A Streetcar Named Desire." New York: New Directions Publishing, 2004. Print.

# MLA Formatting for Your Paper

When writing an academic paper, you are exploring and expressing your ideas about the assigned topic. You need to trust that your instructor has provided you with everything you need to complete the assignment and challenge yourself to rise to the task. If you have engaged with the material and completed brain-storming, you should be in good shape to get started.

If you have surfed the internet to find ideas, you need to consider the ethical use of sources to avoid plagiarism.

*What is wrong with using ideas I find on the internet?*

We all surf the internet to access information; we all use the information we find on the internet in a variety of ways. Sometimes we alter it. Sometimes we summarize it in our own words. Sometimes we copy and paste or print. Regardless of the way we use the stuff we have found on the internet, or any other source outside of our own ideas, we need to give credit to the source. **If you do NOT give credit to your source, you are stealing, or plagiarizing. Plagiarizing is a form of cheating.**

If you were to do a web surf using the words plagiarism and cheating, you would discover that many leading universities and colleges consider plagiarism cheating. Cheating can affect your academic standing and/or the loss of credit. Why not learn a good habit now?

*What constitutes plagiarizing?*

Plagiarism is passing off the ideas (words or images) of someone else as your own.

What are some of the ways students plagiarize?

- Summarizing and paraphrasing — Many students think that it is okay to use someone's ideas as long as you put them in your own words. This is still plagiarism.

**Think about it!** If you were asked to summarize the plot of a movie, say *The Desolation of Smaug*, does that make you JRR Tolkien or Peter Jackson? No, you are describing *their* ideas.

*Solution:* Give the person or source credit for their ideas with a properly formatted MLA citation (more on that later).

- Copy and paste — We all use the copy and paste function on our devices because it saves time; however, unless we give credit to the source, we are stealing or plagiarizing.

**Think about it!** You decide to look and see what *a website* has to say about symbolism of the beast in *Lord of the Flies* because you have an easy due in the morning. You find the perfect thesis: "The beast epitomizes evil; however, does it represent the potential evil in the hearts of every human, or does the beast embody an external tendency to evil or savagery that is held in check by rules and civilization?"

Perfect, right? Wrong! If you look at the information and decide to use it in any form, you need to give credit to your source.

*Solution:*

A great way to use this idea is in your body paragraph about internal and external darkness. You can introduce the quotation by citing the source:

> A piece on *(name that website)* exploring the symbolism of the beast raises some interesting questions while stating that the beast does "epitomize evil; however, does it represent the potential evil in the hearts of every human, or does the beast embody an external tendency to evil or savagery that is held in check by rules and civilization?"

Give the person or source credit for their ideas with a properly formatted MLA citation (more on that later).

## What is MLA?

MLA stands for Modern Language Association, a governing body that oversees many aspects of publishing and academic writing. It publishes a style guide which is updated periodically outlining the correct way to cite sources and format academic papers. MLA is one of many formats. The most current version of MLA is the 7th edition of *MLA Handbook for Writers of Research Papers* published in 2009.

*Do I have to memorize MLA format?*

Your teacher may ask you to learn some basic formats used by MLA. A great resource for all things English, but especially MLA formatting, is OWL — the Online Writing Lab of Purdue University. You should have it bookmarked on your browser.

You should at the very least know how sources are categorized - print and web - and what type of information you need to cite each source.

Here are some basic rules for setting up your document

- One-inch margins on all four sides
- Double spaced
- Indent first line of each paragraph
- Numbered pages in upper-right corner
- Use italics for titles: web sites, book length works or films
- Use quotation marks for titles of poems, short stories, songs or tv shows
- Create a title page ONLY upon request of instructor
- Heading Upper Left corner of first page:

Your Name
Instructor's name
Assignment title
Date

## Get Your Sources Organized

Make giving credit to your sources a priority and begin a new habit of mind. I always start a piece of writing with a working bibliography where I log everything I look at. Here are some ways you can keep track of your sources:

- Take a screen shot of the sources you use so you can find them again.
- Copy and paste urls at the end of your draft, so you can go back to the piece.
  URLS *may not be used as a works cited entry* or a citation.
- Start a working bibliography for every paper you write with the text you are writing about as the first source and an entry for everything else you look at.
- Use your browser history to find "lost" sources.
- Use an online file cabinet: OneNote, Google Find, Evernote, etc.

## Citing Your Sources

*What exactly does "cite" mean? I hear it often but am a little unclear about what it means.*

According to <u>dictionary.com</u>, the word "cite" means
"to quote (a passage, book, author, etc.), especially as an authority" or "to mention in support, proof, or confirmation"

We use cite to mean the use of someone else's ideas in a paper and the attribution of credit to that person/source. So basically, it means the quotation, paraphrase, summary and the in-text or parenthetical reference and the works cited entry.

*In-text citations seem complicated. Is there any way to help make it less complicated?*

One of the easiest ways to keep in-text citations straight is to write your works cited entry first because the words against the margin — the first words in your works cited entry — are the ones that appear in your in-text citation so that your reader can easily find the source you are mentioning in case s/he wants to read it.

The following solutions and examples are based on the assumption that it has been made clear in the introduction or elsewhere in the paper that the work in discussion is *The Tragedy of Hamlet, Prince of Denmark* by William Shakespeare.

- Unless your quotation ends in an exclamation point or a question mark, your end punctuation will always come after the in-text citation's parenthesis.

Example: Hamlet's mother is worried about his depression and resentment toward his uncle, the new king, asking him to "look like a friend on Denmark" (1.2.271).

- If your quotation ends with an exclamation point or a question mark those marks serve as end punctuation — do not use a period after the parenthesis.

Example:  In Act III scene 4, Hamlet greets his obviously upset mother with the words "Now, mother, what is the matter?" (2395)

NOTE: This source begins numbering lines from the beginning without starting new at each act, so simply line numbers will do although providing act and scene numbers would be helpful for your reader.

- If you are discussing one work and have mentioned the tile and author previously, you do not need to include more than the page number or location in your citation.

- If you have introduced your quotation and mentioned the writer/speaker you do not need to include more than the page number or location in your citation.

*What's the difference between a Bibliography and Works Cited or Sources Page?*

A bibliography is a formatted list of all the material you looked at during the research and writing process — whether you use the information or not.  A Works Cited or Sources is a formatted list of everything you paraphrase, summarize or quote in your paper — the things you actually use and give credit to.  There MUST be a direct correlation between Works Cited page and the in-text/parenthetical sources!  In the following examples, I give you a works cited entry and a sample in-text citation.

Works Cited

"Cite." .1 -2. *dictionary.com* Random House Dictionary. 2014. Web. August 2014.

*Purdue OWLFamily of Sites*. "MLA Formatting and Style Guide." 2008. Web. August 2014.

Shakespeare, William. "The Tragedy of Hamlet, Prince of Denmark." *OpenSource Shakespeare.* George Mason University 2013-2014. Web. August 2014.

## MLA Style Guide Basics

MLA Style Guides are generally divided into these four categories for formatting both your quoted material and your works cited page!

Book — print and bound with a single publishing date per edition

Periodical — print and bound with multiple publish dates per year — magazines, newspapers, journals

Electronic — web and database sources which need the use of electronic technology to access

Other — films, recording, interviews and other sources that do not fit into the above 3

**Book by a single author** — Works Cited page and quoted passage

Conroy, Pat. *My Reading Life.* New York: Doubleday, 2010. Print.

It is an irony that "intellectual life often forms in the strangest, most infertile of conditions" (Conroy, 3).

Conroy points out the irony of the writing life that can develop "in the strangest, most infertile of conditions" (3).

**Book in translation** — Works Cited page and quoted passage.

Coehlo, Paulo. *Warrior of the Light: A Manual*. Trans. Margaret Jull
      Costa. New York: HarperCollins Perennial, 2004. Print.

Paul Coehlo draws upon wisdom literature from all cultures. For
example, he includes an idea from the *Tao Te Ching* when he states,
"The Way involves respect for small and subtle things" (26).

Those who struggle to live a deliberate and aware life must nurture a
"combination of discipline and acceptance to fuel his enthusiasm"
(Coehlo, 32).

**Book in a collection or Anthology** — Works Cited page and quoted
passage.

Joyce, James. "Araby." *Dubliners*. New York: Dover Publications,
      Inc., 1991. Print.

James Joyce repeats the word "blind" to underscore his theme that
self-delusion permeates the human experience. For example, Joyce
describes the setting of the story, "North Richmond Street, being blind
was a quiet street" (15).

Writers employ light and dark imagery to establish mood: "The space
of the sky above us was the color of ever-changing violet and towards it
the lamps of the street lifted their feeble lanterns" (Joyce, 15).

The first example mentions James Joyce the author, so the parenthetical
reference/in-text citation lists page number. The second example does
not include the name of the author, so the last name and page number
are given.

IF your book does not fit in any of the above categories, go to a style guide such as OWL, click on Books and scroll through the choices until you find one that matches your need. If you have questions, bring the source to your teacher and ask for help.

**Electronic sources**

The formatting for electronic sources has changed along with the development of search engines such as Google. One of the changes is the use of urls - or copied and pasted web addresses. If you have every tried copy and pasting a url into a document, you can understand the need for change because they always include a hyperlink, often appear in blue and underlined, and can be a nuisance to change.

Also, many students tend to think that providing a url is the correct way to format a works cited entry. WRONG!

**Online Newspaper** — An Article in an Online Magazine

Morris, Loveday. "Iraqi President Names Haider al-Abadi New Prime
      Minister, Defying Maliki. *The Washington Post: Middle East.*
      11 August 2014. Web. 12 August 2014.

Example of in-text citation: The recent announcement naming Haider al-abaci as Iraq's new prime minister may set "the stage for a vicious showdown in a country already struggling to contain an Islamist extremist insurgency" (Morris).

Notice: There is no url because search engine can readily find sources. One could simple type in the author and "Iraqi President" to find the source.

✓ The capitalization in the article is changed to MLA format with all words capitalized except articles and short prepositions — on, in, the an — that are not the first word in an article.

Finding an author, editor, publisher info for a website is possible with a minimum of digging.     Most websites have a banner at the very bottom of the main page that has a link "about us" or "site map." If you click on one of these it should take you to a place that lists the editor or writer of the piece if it is not obvious on the article. Some websites such as blogs are written, edited by the owner.

## An Image (painting, sculpture, photograph)

We all take images from the internet — in fact, the use of internet images is a hot issue in intellectual property and copyright circles. The ethical thing to do is cite your source — correctly.

Let's pretend you are writing a paper about the astronomical accuracy of Van Gogh's painting "Starry Night" and want to include an image of the painting for your reader. You do exactly what any of us would do: google "Starry Night" and click on images. Innumerable image would show up.

The quality of the images varies widely, so as a writer and researcher, I would want to see a photo of the original painting. I would look for one that is associated with a museum and find MoMA — which is the Museum of Modern Art in New York.

I would also know that there are several paintings titled "Starry Night" and this one I want was painted June 1889 in Saint Remy.

Starry Night (1889) by Van Gogh

Use a caption to label your painting in your paper which will serve as an in-text citation.

Works Cited Entry Example

Van Gogh, Vincent. *Starry Night*. 1889. Museum of Modern Art, New York. Web. 12 August 2014.

**Article from a Database**

**What is a database?**   A database is a collection of periodicals, magazines, newspapers and journals, that is stored electronically and is available through a subscription service.  That means that someone has to pay for you to access the collection.  In the case of most students, the library pays for the subscription.   EBSCO and ProQuest are databases.

A rule of thumb is that if you have to access the information through a library using a password, then you are using a database.

Langhamer, Claire. "Love and Courtship in Mid-Twentieth Century England." *Historical Journal* 50.1 (2007): 173 - 96. *Proquest.* Web. 27 May 2009.

Notice the title of the journal and the name of the database are in italics.
50:1 indicates the volume and issue of the journal
173 - 96 indicates the range of pages for the article

Email, tweets and Youtube videos are also electronic sources.

## Formatting a Works Cited Page MLA Style

- Set the margins at one inch
- Center the words Works Cited at the top of the page
- Use hanging indentations — first line of entry against the margin second and each subsequent line indented one tab
- Double space
- Entries are in Alphabetical order
- No bolds
- No urls — this may vary by teacher
- DO NOT number your entries
- If you use a bibliography making source, you still need to adhere to MLA formatting.

SAMPLE

Works Cited

Czlapinski, Becky. "Bagua & My Space." *Tropical Feng Shui Living.* 31 January 2018. Web. 11 January 2018.

Hosseini, Khaled. *The Kite Runner.* New York: Berkley Publishing Group, 2003.

Szymborka, Wistawa. "Brueghel's Two Monkeys." *Wistawa Szymborska: Poems New and Collected.* Trans. Stanislaw Baranczak and Clare Cavanaugh. New York: Harcourt, Inc., 1999.

Printed in Great Britain
by Amazon

27674555R00061